Shell Life on the Seashore

Shell Life
on the Seashore

PHILIP STREET

Illustrated by
NOEL GREGORY

FABER & FABER

First published in 1961 by Faber & Faber Limited

This new edition published in 2019
by Faber & Faber Ltd
Bloomsbury House
74–77 Great Russell Street
London WC1B 3DA
First published in the USA in 2019

Typeset by Faber & Faber Ltd
Printed and bound in the UK by TJ International Ltd, Padstow, Cornwall

The publishers are grateful to Helen Scales for her
assistance in updating the text.

A CIP record for this book
is available from the British Library

ISBN 978–0–571–35445–0

FSC
www.fsc.org
MIX
Paper from
responsible sources
FSC® C013056

2 4 6 8 10 9 7 5 3 1

Dedicated with good wishes
to
John and Doolet

Contents

Illustrations

Foreword

by Philip Hoare

The shore is the last and first place. It's where we began, and where evolution is still visibly underway. A remote zone on our doorstep, an exotic jungle revealed and concealed twice a day, the intertidal zone draws us to itself as a memory of our own watery origins.

And yet its plants and animals seem utterly other. Strange, alien things with radulas and enormous feet and more than the requisite number of legs or eyes, gripping and clasping and rasping, delicately picking their way over a terrain that seems as transformative as them. These bizarre life forms that seem simple and complex at the same time: both fragile – what lies beneath shells and suckers and spines – and intensely tough, able to withstand the greatest storms that would fell our puny bodies into submission.

Down there is a microscopic world to which our eyes were attuned as children. We may as well have been looking down the wrong end of a telescope to another planet. We knew then that this could be anything, this other world in a rock pool, a puddle, or a foreshore.

Shakespeare knew as much; his sprite Ariel, in *The Tempest*, sings a song that transforms into those creatures.

> Of his bones are coral made;
> Those are pearls that were his eyes;
> Nothing of him that doth fade,
> But doth suffer a sea-change
> Into something rich and strange.

People around the world and throughout time have ascribed magical powers to shellfish. In the creation myth of the Haida people of the Northwest Pacific, the first humans crawled out of an oyster inseminated by the trickster Raven as a joke. In New Zealand the Māori revere the iridescence of the pāua shell as the eyes of their ancestors in the stars.

It's not hard to see why these part-animal, part-plant, part-stone things accrue myth and legend, along with their shells. They are elusive and cryptic: the shimmer inside a mussel, while its exterior seems to be made of steely blue; the nacre of an oyster, lustrous and smooth yet mineral-hard; the gothic whorls of a topshell, spiralling up out of the mud towards the sky. They're as much architecture as animals: fractal constructions, whirling microcosms. Other worlds, an inch long.

None of this is to be expected, for all that it is familiar, this litter on the shore. It is what is left behind, empty yet subtly full of life, in and of the water and apart from it, waiting to be gathered up, by the tide, by the birds, by us. It is the sea at our feet and the sea inside. There's a good reason why we remember it. We humans climbed out of the trees and onto the shore to gather shellfish whose omega oils helped our brains to grow. Atavistically, we're drawn back there; far from danger, this incoming sea represents sustenance and survival.

In his intrepid survey, Philip Street peers down into that edge for us; he crouches on the beach and sees not one but 'a whole series of habitats', teeming with life. Street estimates 40,000 animals may live in each square yard of bladder wrack. And those inhabitants manage their survival through constancy and change; their liminal environment necessitates adaptation, covered and exposed as they are. Shelled things defy our presumptions by moving speedily when we're not looking. They're true shape-shifters. The limpets hold fast to rocks. Periwinkles survive without sea water for months. 'They are, in fact, in the adult stage, almost land animals . . .' says Street, 'gradually being modified so that they too, in time, may well be able to leave the shore altogether and take up a purely terrestrial existence.' The Precambrian turns into the future.

Street reassures us of our own inconsequentiality. His exacting descriptions spark off extraordinary scenes. I find intensely moving his account of the turf of carrageen moss that grows on a winkle; a green bouquet sported, then ripped off as the animal is readied for market and human consumption. He also tells us of the mussel larvae that flourished after the Dutch island of Walcheren was flooded in the Allied bombing of 1944. For a year the land was inundated by the North Sea; a year later, when the water was pumped away, the islanders discovered that mussels had begun to grow on the walls of their houses, their fences, and even on the trees. It's an image that evokes the medieval belief that barnacle geese hatched out of shellfish. It also reminds me of *Moby-Dick* and Herman Melville's chapter on Nantucket, an island which the author had then yet to visit, but which he described as so watery that 'to their very chairs and tables small clams will sometimes be found adhering, as to the backs of turtles'.

Street wanders into his lovely detail, waylaying us with these anecdotes as we beachcomb. He tells us that painter's mussels, a freshwater variety, provided Dutch painters with receptacles for their pigments and even gold and silver leaf; which in turn makes me wonder if these shells auditioned for this precious role by displaying their silky silver lining. To me, they're reminders of Rembrandt, who collected shells for their aesthetic sake and called them 'God's handiwork'. The modern Surrealists would turn their strangeness into art too, in the collages and sculptures of Max Ernst and Eileen Agar and the paintings of Edward Wadsworth and Paul Nash, imposing giant shells as monstrous interruptions into ordinary life. It is a fanciful eeriness also reflected in the concrete shell gardens once common in interwar seaside suburbs; an outsider art as a modest echo of the eighteenth-century fashion for gloomy shell-studded grottos.

As Street sorts out the vegetarian snails from the carnivorous snails, I can't help but wonder at the unimaginable: what might it be like to be a shellfish? To be at the feet of everyone. Hidden in their carapaces like the creatures that live inside Daleks, many possess a single foot, and – needing little sensory input, as Street says – have not bothered to grow heads. Very economical of them. Conversely, perhaps even perversely, their stomachs are external. No surrealist could invent anything that strange.

Memorably, and almost indelicately, Street describes sea-slugs as naked snails; while the most common shellfish acquire entire other meanings in this queer edge of the sea, neither one place nor another. The familiar slipper limpet, he reveals, is another invader, brought over from America a century ago. (According to the National Oceanographic Centre, my local shore, Southampton Water, is home to the highest number of alien organisms in British waters, filled with migrants that arrived on or in foreign ships.) This sly slipper shifter clusters in towers of itself, each piggy-backing on the other in a gendered hierarchy: the lowest are females, the top two or three are young males. Yet those in between really are in between – in the process of changing from one sex to another, from male to female. They're a shellfish matriarchy enacted in slow motion, these molluscan Orlandos.

Shells stand the test and sense of time. They challenge natural history and mortality in the manner in which they preserve their own beautiful carapaces, these hard products of creatures so sensually soft. The shiny gloss on a cowrie is maintained by the mantle that the living animal wraps over itself, like a slithery duvet, conserving a veneer more luxurious than any piece of lovingly polished Chippendale furniture. But they can also be deadly, if poisoned by the algae blooms of a red tide, becoming bearers of a fatal toxin for unsuspecting humans.

Each of these shells receives its own moment in the sun in Street's book, brought onstage for their performance, mortal or otherwise. They are turned around in his fingers, examined from every angle, both inside and out, accorded their virtues and values, as far as we humans are concerned. In the Outer Hebrides people relied on cockles to survive, much as Mark Kurlansky tells us in his book, *The Big Oyster*, the inhabitants of Manhattan were said never to have suffered hunger in the past, since there was always a ready supply of oysters, as the city's archaeological middens indicate. I wonder if the Hebrideans counted the dark rings on their rayed shells, the method by which Street teaches us to age them, telling off each year like a tree? If you might hear the infinite sea through a tiny shell, why shouldn't it become a kind of calendar? Native Americans, like other indigenous people, used shells as hard currency, as if in acknowledgement of the intrinsic value of their beauty.

But beyond their utility to us, persistence is the shellfish's cardinal quality. It is the engine of its survival. Those sand-dwelling cockles, hiding in the sand, unattached to rocks, sea walls or groynes like their tethered shellfish peers, are among the most successful of their kind, Street says. They endure in the sharp clattery piles of them that I find after my daily swims. The scallop, too, declared independence, as it discovered it was able to shoot itself across the sea bed with its jet of water sent out through its valves. It seems apt that this wandering mollusc became the symbol of human pilgrimage through its association with St James, the fisherman, and Santiago de Compostela, the site of his shrine.

Street's measured narrative – inching along the shore, minding tide and time – excels itself on the subject of the oyster. The native oyster is a slender, subtle, encrusted creature, and the author points out that its cultivation is relatively recent; at the time of Street's writing, its farming was confined to Colchester, Whitstable, and the Helford river in Cornwall. Nowadays you are more likely to encounter the pumped-up Pacific oyster on a British shore. Yet these incomers clean our polluted waters, like other filterers, performing jobs we would rather not do. And once eaten, their shells ought to be cast back into the sea, since there their zooplankton progeny, called spats, can fasten themselves to their ancestors' carapaces and grow apace to continue the cycle of consumption. But I'm afraid I can't help thinking of Lewis Carroll's Walrus and Carpenter, out for a walk with their oyster friends.

> 'O Oysters,' said the Carpenter,
> 'You've had a pleasant run!
> Shall we be trotting home again?'
> But answer came there none –
> And this was scarcely odd, because
> They'd eaten every one.

'I like the Walrus best', says Alice, 'because you see he was a little sorry for the oysters.' And when out clamming with my friend Dennis Minsky on the low tide of a New England beach, he always does them honour when we take them back for dinner, saying, 'Sorry little brother', as he puts each one into the pot.

And so Street's book moves towards its many-armed finale, as he includes the cephalopods – octopuses, squids and cuttlefishes – as the ultimate molluscs. The cuttlebones we find like some slice of styrofoam in the wrackline were once ground down to blot up the very ink that they supplied, as their taxonomic name, *Sepia*, commemorates. Meanwhile the octopus that Street describes cracking open crabs and lobsters like some mini Kraken has turned around in modern biology to become an animal we now know to have the intelligence of a three-year-old human, with arms that possess individual brains. It is truly an extraterrestrial that has slipped its shell.

Armed with Street's book, we can see a brave new world down there on the beach. Not the slimy things that affrighted the Ancient Mariner, nor something to be served up on a plate, but beautiful animals deserving of our scrutiny, demanding that we get down on our knees. Our reward for this worship? Exquisite revelation, of the most wonderful, watery kind.

Introduction

Many people who go to the seaside for their holidays become interested in the great variety and abundance of animal life found on the shore. Particularly attractive to them are the shells left behind on the beach by the receding tide. There is a fascination in their great variety of form and colour, and many a returning holidaymaker's luggage will contain a small collection of these shells gathered from the beach.

Generally, however, these shells remain a mystery, and the collector little suspects the interesting lives led by the animals that once occupied the shells. Yet each shell has a story to tell if only one knew the language. We can tell not only what kind of animal once lived in it, but also the conditions under which it lived and the problems it had to solve.

Shell Life on the Seashore aims to provide for the enthusiastic amateur and the potential collector a book that will give them the information they need to make shells intelligible to them, by describing the modes of life of the animals and correlating these with the structural features of their shells.

Shells that are found on the beach come from several different sources. Many of them belong to seashore animals living among the seaweeds and on the rocks, and these will nearly always be found complete with their occupants. A few belong to burrowing animals that live buried unsuspected in the sand or mud over which we walk. These are usually found on the surface only after their occupants have died, washed up from below by the force of the waves, and usually empty. A considerable proportion, too, belong to true marine molluscs, which live beyond the low-tide mark either on the sea bed or buried in it. These also will only be cast upon the beach as empties after their occupants have died or have been eaten.

Although shell-bearing animals are most abundant on the shore and in the sea, they have important relatives on land and in ponds, and any shell collector will probably turn their attention to these sooner or later. A few passages dealing with these, and showing how they have been derived from seashore ancestors, will be included.

The animals that occupy these various shells belong to one of the largest and most successful groups of invertebrates, the Mollusca. Their bodies are soft, lacking any kind of internal supporting skeleton, but relying instead upon the external calcareous shell. There are three main types of molluscs: those with a single, usually coiled shell, of which the various kinds of terrestrial and marine snails are typical; those with a shell consisting of two halves or valves joined together by ligaments, represented by animals like mussels and oysters; and the most highly developed group of all, the octopuses and squids, in which the ancestral coiled shell has become internal and much reduced, or lost altogether. In addition there are smaller groups, represented only by a few animals, which are important because they occupy intermediate positions between the larger groups and indicate the probable lines of evolution within the group as a whole.

Although the seashore is so teeming with life that you can find a greater variety of animals there than in any area of comparable size on land, conditions are very exacting, due to the effects of the tides. Elsewhere an animal is either terrestrial, spending its whole life exposed to the air, or it is aquatic, being all the time in water. Only on the shore must animals spend part of each day as terrestrial creatures and the remainder as aquatic. They must be adapted to a greater range of conditions than any other animals.

The main problems they have to contend with are to avoid becoming dried up when left uncovered by the receding tide, especially in hot sunny weather; to be able to breathe both in air and in water; to be able to breed and feed satisfactorily; and to be able to resist the pounding action of the waves as the tide passes to and fro over them, especially in heavy seas. All the shore molluscs, as we shall see, are modified both in their structure and their behaviour to enable them to cope with these various problems.

The seashore, too, is not a uniform habitat where a certain set of conditions occur. Rather it is a whole series of habitats, each imposing its own set of problems to be solved by any animal that chooses to live there, and each therefore having its own population of animals so adapted as to be able to cope with them.

Even on the same shore, conditions vary from one part to another. Molluscs that live high up on the shore will be underwater for much shorter periods than those lower down the shore, and will consequently have to be better adapted to endure the effects of exposure to air. Each species has its own optimum periods of immersion and exposure, and will thus tend to be found only in that region of the shore where these conditions prevail. Hence it is that seashore animals are zoned, each animal occupying the area where conditions are best suited to it. When you are searching for molluscs on the shore a knowledge of these zones will be a great help. Fortunately the larger seaweeds are similarly zoned, and since they are more conspicuous than the shore animals, they are valuable as zone indicators.

Shores as a whole can differ from one another in their conditions, and therefore can have distinctive populations. Many of the molluscs found on a rocky shore could not survive on one which was muddy. Sandy and stony shores will likewise have their own populations.

The extent to which a shore is exposed to waves can

also affect the distribution of shore animals, some preferring an exposed beach while others are unable to survive
very rough seas. The mollusc population of a sheltered
beach may therefore differ significantly from that of one
subjected to the full force of waves coming in from the
open sea. Sometimes these differences can be seen on two
adjacent beaches separated by a headland which provides
shelter for the one while leaving the other unprotected.

Geographical position, too, plays an important part
in the distribution both of marine and seashore animals.
They are nearly all very sensitive to temperature, each
having its own optimum temperature range. Thus the
mollusc populations of two similar beaches and their
offshore waters in the south-west of England and the
north-east of Scotland will differ considerably.

The distribution of seaweeds, too, plays an important part in determining the allocation of animals. Some
shore molluscs rely on the protection seaweeds afford
from the heating and drying effects of the sun's rays, hiding among the damp fronds until the tide returns; others
can only live on rocks where no seaweeds are present.

Another important factor affecting the distribution
of shore molluscs is the rock pool. On whatever part of
the shore it occurs, the conditions for life in it differ considerably from those of the surrounding areas. Because
there is always water available, many animals can live
much higher on the shore in the vicinity of a rock pool

than they could do normally. Certain species cannot live on the shore at all except in these pools. Even a cursory glance into a pool may show many kinds of molluscs on the bottom and sides, often in considerable numbers. Many others can be found by turning over the loose stones which often cover the bottom of the pool. If, however, you do turn a stone, replace it right-way up when you have examined its under-surface, because any animals you find there are relying on the stone for shelter. To leave them exposed makes them easy prey for their enemies.

One of the features of shore- and marine-animal life is the large number of animals that lead a fixed or sedentary existence, permanently attached to rocks or stones. On land, conditions do not lend themselves to sedentary life for animals, but on the shore and in the seas some of the most successful forms of animal life are sedentary. Among the molluscs we find that many of those with bivalve shells are extremely well adapted both in structure and behaviour to such an existence.

The best time to look for shore molluscs is at low tide, when the maximum area of beach is uncovered. Many species are only found low down on the beach, because they cannot survive exposure to the air for very long. Spring tides are particularly favourable for shore work, because the water both goes out and comes in further than it does at other times. Low spring tides thus expose rocks that remain covered even at low tide at other times. Spring tides occur for a few days each fortnight, coin-ciding with full moon and new moon. Those that occur during the intervening period are known as neap tides.

It is in their adaptations for feeding, breathing and reproduction that the seashore and marine molluscs show their most important modifications, and it is to these three important functions that we shall have to refer frequently in order to understand the lives of the animals that live in the shells.

Broadly speaking, all molluscs adopt one of three methods of feeding. Some are vegetarian, rasping mouth-fuls of seaweed with their special toothed feeding ribbon, the radula. Others are carnivorous, using the radula first to bore through the shells of other molluscs and then to devour the soft bodies within. A very large number, however, exist entirely on the minute plankton that live suspended in the sea water, using specially modified gills to filter these organisms from the respiratory current of water that is constantly being drawn into and through the gill cavity.

Gills of one kind or another are universally employed for extracting the necessary oxygen from the surround-ing sea water. Essentially a gill is an organ in which considerable quantities of blood run in numerous tiny thin-walled blood-vessels all over the surface, so that blood and sea water are separated only by the thinnest layers of tissue. Oxygen can thus pass readily from water to blood, and waste carbon dioxide in the reverse direction. Usually a respiratory current of water is drawn into the gill cavity and passed over the gills, often being used as a food current as well, as previously mentioned. Respiratory currents are usually set up by the gills themselves, which are covered with minute hair-like processes capable of rhythmic beating so as to keep the water always flowing in one direction.

In their methods of reproduction a majority of the molluscs adopt a system which is common to many marine and seashore animals. Male and female reproductive products are merely shed into the sea, usually with no form of preliminary mating between the sexes, and fertilisation of the eggs by the spermatozoa is a random process. There is usually, however, some mechanism to ensure that the majority of individuals of a particular species in the same area all spawn into the sea roughly simultaneously, so that there will at this time be a high concentration of reproductive products in the water, and in consequence the majority of eggs will be fertilised.

From the eggs tiny larvae of microscopic size hatch out. These are generally quite unlike their parents either in structure or habits, and spend the first few weeks of their lives floating and drifting in the surface waters as members of the plankton. During the spring and summer, in fact, a considerable proportion of the plankton consists of the developing eggs and larvae of all kinds of marine creatures. Many of the eggs will provide food for other animals in the plankton before they have had an opportunity to hatch, and many of the larvae that do eventually hatch out will share the same fate.

Eventually these larvae, after feeding hard and growing fast, change to the adult form and sink down on to the sea bed or on to the shore when the tide is in. This settling is of course quite haphazard, so that some will fall on sand, some on mud and some on rocks or stones. The great majority are doomed to die, for only those which settle on the right kind of ground and, if they are shore animals, in the right zone, will survive.

This may seem a very wasteful method of reproduction and distribution, and certainly explains why marine creatures generally produce such enormous numbers of eggs. Yet it has considerable advantages. Since there are so many larvae, some are almost bound to settle on and occupy suitable vacant spots. So great is the competition for suitable space that such spots may be few and far between. At the same time overcrowding of the parental habitat is avoided.

Not all molluscs, however, adopt this broadcast method of reproduction and dispersal. Quite a number produce egg capsules, each containing a quantity of eggs, and these are usually fixed to rocks or weeds, the young molluscs or mollusc larvae making their way out of these capsules after an initial period of development. A few are viviparous, the females retaining the eggs within their bodies until they have hatched out. The hazards in these two methods are much less than in the broadcast method, so fewer eggs are produced because a greater proportion of them will survive.

Before beginning our detailed study of the shell life of the shore, it will be a considerable advantage to look at the shore seaweeds, because, as mentioned earlier, they are extremely valuable as indicators of the different shore zones and are therefore a great help in showing us where to look for various species.

There are four main groups of seaweeds, or algae: the blue-green, green, red and brown. All the larger shore weeds belong to the last group, and are commonly referred to as wracks. Algae are not differentiated into roots, stems and leaves like other plants. The body of a wrack consists of numerous fronds, anchored to the rocks by means of a holdfast.

At the extreme top of the shore, occupying a narrow zone beyond the reach of the neap tides, is the smallest of the wracks, channelled wrack (*Pelvetia canaliculata*). The whole plant is only a few centimetres long, and its name is derived from its narrow fronds, which are grooved or channelled along one side. Only for a few days each fortnight, during spring tides, does the sea reach these channelled-wrack plants, which must therefore have considerable capacity for resisting desiccation when exposed to the air.

Just down-shore from the channelled-wrack zone is a somewhat wide zone occupied by flat wrack (*Fucus spiralis*), whose short flat fronds have a prominent mid-rib but no air bladders. The fronds are fairly short, but longer than those of the channelled wrack, and it covers the rocks much more densely. This flat-wrack zone extends some way below the neap tide high-water mark.

We now come to a wide zone comprising the whole middle part of the shore, and here we find two wrack species sharing suitable rock surfaces, bladder wrack (*Fucus vesiculosus*) and knotted wrack (*Ascophyllum nodosum*), both with very long fronds up to sixty centimetres in length. The former is the familiar 'pop-weed', with its pairs of air bladders that can be popped lying at intervals along the flat fronds on either side of the prominent mid-rib. Knotted-wrack fronds are thin and round but often much longer than those of bladder wrack and carrying numerous small lateral fronds. At intervals there are single large air bladders much wider than the fronds.

The air bladders serve to suspend the fronds vertically in the water when the tide covers these wracks, bringing them nearer the surface, where more sunlight penetrates. Although these two wracks occupy the same zone, on any shore one or other of them usually predominates. The reason for this is that bladder wrack, with its tougher fronds, is better able to survive heavy seas than knotted wrack. It is therefore more common on exposed beaches, knotted wrack occurring more under sheltered conditions, where for some reason bladder wrack does not appear to do so well. A rocky headland will sometimes have mainly bladder wrack on the exposed side and knotted wrack mainly on the sheltered side. When the two species do occur in equal abundance on the same shore they do not always mingle, but often occupy distinct parts of the general zone. In these circumstances knotted wrack sometimes occurs above bladder wrack, and sometimes below it. Why they should be separated in this way is not known.

The lowest zone on the shore is occupied by serrated wrack (*Fucus serratus*), whose numerous flat fronds with their serrated edges form a dense slippery covering to the rocks on the lower part of the shore. Serrated wrack is easily distinguished from bladder wrack and knotted wrack because it lacks air bladders, and its fronds are much longer than those of flat wrack, which in any case would never be found so far down the shore.

At the extreme low-water mark and extending into the shallow water beyond is the *Laminaria* zone, occupied by the great flat strap-like fronds of *Laminaria digitata*, or tangleweed.

Both the fronds and the sturdy, much-branched holdfast provide attachment and shelter for a number of molluscs and their eggs, which can often be found by searching among *Laminaria* plants torn from their moorings in stormy weather and cast up on the shore.

Each wrack species has its own characteristic animal population, though many animals are found sheltering among the fronds of more than one species. On a well-populated shore the total animal populations of these wracks can reach astounding proportions, 40,000 individuals having been counted on one square yard of bladder wrack. Many of these were of course microscopic in size, but even so it is an astonishing figure, especially when one reflects that without the shelter provided by the plants, the majority of these animals could probably not survive on the shore.

1

The Limpet and Other Shore Gastropods

Perhaps the best known and certainly one of the most common of the single-shelled or gastropod molluscs found on the shore is the limpet. Although, unlike most gastropods, its shell is not coiled, in other respects it is admirably suited to serve as an introduction to the group as a whole, and in its natural history it shows a well-nigh perfect adaptation to life on the seashore.

Detached from the rock to which it normally clings so firmly, and looked at from underneath, the common limpet (*Patella vulgata*) shows typical snail structure.

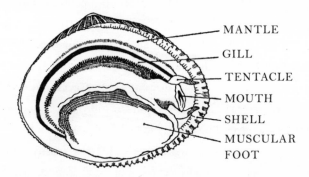

COMMON LIMPET *Patella vulgata* – Ventral view

FIG. 1: × 0.75 NATURAL SIZE

Most of this under-surface consists of a broad muscular foot, by contracting which the limpet is able to glide smoothly over the rocks, in just the same way as a land snail crawls over the ground. Bands of muscle run upwards to attach the foot to the shell. In front of the foot is a small head, complete with a pair of tiny tentacles, and a mouth that opens downwards so as to face the surface over which it passes.

Above the foot is the body proper, or visceral hump, containing all the internal organs and occupying practically the whole of the space in the upper part of the shell. Draped over and attached to this visceral mass, and falling like a continuous curtain all round the head and foot, is a sheet of tissue called the mantle, the function of which is to lay down the original shell in the young animal and add to it as it grows.

Suspended from the roof of the mouth cavity is a second curtain or fringe of tissue. This is the gill, through which oxygen is absorbed from the sea water. This kind of gill is not typical of gastropods in general, most of them having one or a pair of separate plume gills or ctenidia. This fringe gill differs from the separate gills that most other gastropods have. The space enclosed between the foot and this lower part of the mantle is called the mantle cavity, which in the limpet takes the form of a continuous groove.

Mollusc shell is laid down by the mantle in three separate layers. The first and outermost layer consists of horny material. Beneath this a crystalline calcareous layer is then secreted, and the whole finally lined with a smooth, highly polished layer which will remain in immediate contact with the mantle.

Instead of using jaws to eat, the limpet, in common with all other gastropods, employs a remarkable structure called the radula. This consists essentially of a long ribbon set with more than two thousand minute teeth arranged in several rows. The radula is normally withdrawn within the mouth cavity, but whenever the creature feeds it is protruded through the mouth and scraped backwards and forwards, the tiny pieces of food rasped off in this way passing back into the mouth to be swallowed. The radula grows continually throughout the life of the animal, and as the teeth on the front part wear out, the next section, containing new teeth, moves up to replace it.

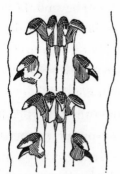

Part of the radula
of the Common Limpet

FIG. 2: APPROX. × 100 NATURAL SIZE

The conical shape of the shell is ideal for an animal exposed to the full force of the waves, offering the least possible resistance to them. It has also made possible the development of a particularly large foot with which the creature is able to maintain its hold even in the stormiest seas. It is not without significance that certain other gastropods whose habits expose them to equally powerful waves have independently acquired a similar conical shell.

A limpet varies the strength of its hold on the rock according to circumstances. When the tide goes out and leaves it exposed it usually relaxes its grip so that the shell is raised slightly above the rock surface, unless the sun is very powerful, in which case it may remain clamped well down. As the tide comes in again it reacts to the first waves that wash gently over it by tightening its grip, and continues to hold on firmly until it is well covered with water and beyond the action of the waves.

A limpet that is relaxed can be detached by giving it a sharp blow or kick, but if it is first gently tapped it will immediately tighten its grip so that a kick violent enough to break its shell will not dislodge it. The gentle tap, like the first waves when the tide is coming in, serves as a warning. Gulls and oyster catchers, the limpet's chief enemies, can only dislodge it when it is relaxed. The gull gives a powerful sideways blow with its beak, while the oyster catcher pushes its beak below the shell margin and prises it off the rock. Both birds seem to know that they can do nothing with a limpet that is clamped tightly to the rock. They will wait patiently until they see one relax its hold and raise its shell.

Limpets cling so tightly to rocks that a pull of thirty kilograms or more may be necessary to remove them. The foot acts as a sucker, being partially retracted in the centre to create a vacuum. When limpets stay in the same spot for a few hours they form an even stronger attachment, gluing themselves in place with a gummy slime which allows them to slide along but makes them very difficult to pull off. Limpets probably alternate between using suction and glue, depending on whether they need to move.

There is an interesting correlation between the position of a limpet on the shore and the shape of its shell. Those living on exposed rocks tend to have taller shells with narrower bases than those living in the shelter of rock pools. The explanation for these differences seems to be connected with the frequency with which the limpet is forced to grip the rocks tightly. Whenever it does so the mantle is pulled inwards, and if this happens frequently it is thought to have the effect of causing the shell to be laid down in a circle of rather smaller diameter than is the case with a mantle that is only pulled inwards occasionally.

No feature shows the limpet's high degree of adaptation to shore life better than its breathing arrangements.

Its ancestors, which lived in the sea and not on the shore, possessed the usual pair of feather-shaped plume gills which are typical of the gastropods. These have been replaced in the modern limpet by the single continuous gill, which is extremely efficient. When the tide goes out a small amount of water is retained within the mantle cavity, and this new gill is able to extract sufficient oxygen from it. Even when relaxed, a limpet will not raise its shell far enough to allow this water to run out. By retaining this water, the limpet also prevents its body from drying out while it is exposed to the air.

Only when it is covered with water does a limpet become active, though in dull or damp weather it may sometimes move about while the tide is out. Unless the sea is very rough, it raises its shell after the incoming tide has swept over it, and glides away in search of food. Like many other shore gastropods it is a vegetarian, feeding on small seaweed sporelings which develop from spores that settle on the rocks. On soft rock scratch marks caused by the limpet's radula as it scrapes off these sporelings can sometimes be seen.

By feeding on these sporelings the shore limpets play an important part in limiting the spread of seaweeds. If there were no limpets, the mid-shore rocks would soon become completely covered with weed, and there would be no room for other animals, like acorn barnacles and mussels, to establish themselves. At the same time, limpets cannot colonise areas where seaweeds are already established, the limpet larvae being swept away by the seaweed fronds as they wave about in the water.

It may seem surprising that an animal that apparently spends much of its time clamped tightly to rocks actually has a well-developed homing instinct and sense of direction. It is a fact, though, that when it has finished feeding it always returns to its original position on the rock, where its foot fits into a shallow depression and the edge of its shell conforms exactly to any irregularities of the rock surface. This conformity is probably produced by mutual wear between rock and shell.

Limpets adopt the broadcast method of breeding so common among marine and seashore life. They spawn during winter, the larvae drifting through the sea for between two and ten days. In that time, the limpet larvae may encounter suitable substrate to settle onto and metamorphose into tiny versions of adult limpets; ideally, they need to settle onto rocks free from seaweeds to stand any chance of survival. It is believed that limpets, like oysters and certain other molluscs, can change their sex during the course of their lives, because nearly all young limpets are males, while older ones are nearly all females.

Besides *Patella vulgata*, which occurs in abundance all around the coasts of Britain, there are two other closely related British species: *Patella depressa* and *Patella ulyssiponensis*. These are very difficult to distinguish from their shells alone. The three species do, however, have different coloured feet: *P. vulgata* has a greenish, grey foot; *P. depressa* has a dark, grey-black foot; and *P. ulyssiponensis* has an apricot-coloured foot.

Less well known than the *P. vulgata* species are several smaller kinds of limpets confined to the lower parts of the shore and extending beyond the low-tide mark. They are all recognisable as limpets on account of their uncoiled shells. Of these other species the one most closely related to *P. vulgata* is the blue-rayed limpet, *P. pellucida*, whose habits and shell colour both change as it grows older. Young specimens have beautiful yellowish-brown translucent shells crossed by a number of bright blue stripes. They are generally to be found clinging to the big strap-like fronds of the *Laminaria* seaweed, which occurs just above and below the low-tide mark. Their very flattened shells, about six millimetres long, enable the animals to retain their hold while the fronds are waved to and fro by the constant movements of the water.

As the blue-rayed limpet grows larger, its shell darkens and becomes taller. It then migrates down the frond to the holdfast at the base of the seaweed, where it proceeds to excavate a shallow depression in which it will spend the remainder of its life sheltered from the effects of water movement.

Two other small limpets found clinging to the undersurface of stones in the *Laminaria* zone well down the shore are the tortoiseshell limpet, *Testudinalia testudi-nalis,* and the closely related white tortoiseshell limpet, *Tectura virginea.* Both have patterned shells up to about thirteen millimetres long, the former being mainly grey-ish brown and the latter yellowish white or pink. They are less specialised animals than *Patella,* still retaining one of the ancestral plumed gills and having developed no fringe gill.

Young form

Older form

BLUE-RAYED LIMPET
Patella pellucida

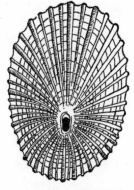

KEYHOLE LIMPET
Diadora graeca

COAT-OF-MAIL SHELL
Lepidochitona cinerea

FIG. 3: BLUE-RAYED LIMPET: ×1.5 NATURAL SIZE;
KEYHOLE LIMPET AND COAT-OF-MAIL SHELL: BOTH NATURAL

The last of our limpets is the keyhole limpet, *Diodora graeca.* Not only has it an uncoiled shell like all the other limpets, but it has also retained both of the ancestral plumed gills. Its most characteristic feature is an oval slit or 'keyhole' in the top of the shell, which approaches 1.25 centimetres in length in a full-grown specimen. In common with all other limpets that have not developed a fringe gill, it is confined to the lower parts of the shore, where it is only exposed to the air for short periods at a time. It is usually found attached to stones.

As well as the British species of limpets mentioned here, there are many other gastropods that have a similar-looking volcano-shaped shell and a large foot. A study of living and extinct fossil gastropods found that molluscs with limpet-like shells have evolved at least fifty-four times separately, and each time they evolved from ancestors with coiled shells. There is even one group in which a snail with a limpet-shaped shell re-evolved a coiled shell, something that was thought to be an evolutionary impossibility. The fact that molluscs have evolved limpet-like shells over and over again shows that this arrangement must be highly advantageous, offering them the ability to hold on tight to rocks and withstand waves and intruding predators.

Another group of molluscs that live a similar life to limpets, clamped tightly to rocks, are the chitons or coat-of-mail shells, which form a separate class, the Polyplacophora. Chitons first evolved at least 500 million years ago, in the Late Cambrian period, and since then they have not changed a great deal in their appearance.

Roughly twenty-five million years ago, chitons evolved hundreds of simple eyes, known as ocelli, embedded in their shell plates. Unlike all other animals which make the lenses in their eyes from protein, chitons have lenses made from the mineral aragonite, a version of calcium carbonate. In 2011, scientists at Duke University in the United States showed that one chiton species, the West Indian fuzzy chiton (*Acanthopleura granulata*), is capable of forming simple images with its eyes. In laboratory tests, the seven-centimetre-long chitons responded to the sudden appearance of black overhead circles ranging from 0.35 centimetres to ten centimetres in diameter. It also seems that chitons can see both in water and in air.

Chitons are usually found clinging to the under-surface of stones well down the shore. There are about half a dozen species, none of which usually exceeds two centimetres in length. If a chiton does become detached, it is able to roll itself up into a ball like a woodlouse. Presumably this protects it from injury while it is being rolled about by the movements of the water. Like the limpets, chitons are vegetarians, scraping minute seaweed sporelings off the rocks with their radulas.

Examination of the internal structure of a limpet, and especially of its nervous system, shows that its whole visceral hump has twisted through an angle of 180 degrees. This twisting is known as torsion (it is not the same thing as the spiralling of the coiled shell in many gastropods).

Viewed from the top, torsion takes place in an anti-clockwise direction. It means that the mantle cavity, ctenidia and the various openings, including the anus, have come to lie towards the front of the animal, above its head.

Valuable evidence that torsion has taken place is provided in the life history of gastropods. In the larvae there is no torsion – gills, mantle cavity and anus being at the hind end of the body. But at a certain stage in the development of Patellogastropoda (the true limpets, such as the common limpet) and Vetigastropoda (the ancient lineage of sea snails that includes the keyhole limpet) the visceral hump begins to twist, these structures being turned through 180 degrees until they come to the front end of the animal. This twisting can actually be observed taking place before your eyes, and in some species it is completed in a period of a few minutes.

In some gastropod groups there is secondary detorsion, or untwisting back towards the original position. Gastropods that undergo partial or complete detorsion include various types of sea-slugs, such as sacoglossans and nudibranchs, and air-breathing slugs and snails, such as Stylommatophora and Orthurethra.

Exactly why torsion originally evolved in gastropods is still not well understood. One possibility for this contorted anatomy is that by moving the mantle cavity over the head, the gastropod can withdraw its head into its shell and protect itself when predators attack.

2

Winkles, Top Shells and Their Relatives

The common periwinkle and its three related species, the small, rough and flat periwinkles, between them provide one of the best examples of zoning on the seashore. Each is adapted for life on a certain part of the shore, and its behaviour pattern is so constituted as to cause it to remain within its zone and to move back to it if it is displaced.

As explained in the Introduction, the main factors which decide on what part of the shore an animal can live satisfactorily are on the one hand its ability to breathe air and to avoid being dried up when the tide is out, and on the other its ability to endure immersion in the sea, which for many shore animals is as serious a problem as avoiding desiccation.

The four periwinkles all differ in their ability to survive these conditions, and are in consequence found occupying four different zones. Highest of all comes the small periwinkle (*Melarhaphe neritoides*), which is found mainly at and a little beyond the extreme range of high spring tides, in what is called the splash zone. Except during the winter storms, when the spring tides are particularly high, the only sea water the majority of the small periwinkles get is splashed onto them from the spring-tide surf once a fortnight. They are very tiny periwinkles, averaging about three millimetres in length, and usually found congregated in small crevices in the rocks around the high-tide mark. They are often mistaken for young common winkles, which would not, however, be able to survive so high on the shore.

The rough periwinkle, *Littorina saxatilis*, is not quite so well able to resist desiccation as the small periwinkle, but it does occur high on the shore, extending almost into the splash zone from some way down the shore. It is a much larger animal, nearly as large as the common periwinkle when full grown, and attractive yellow specimens are quite common. Like the small periwinkle, it prefers weed-free rocks, and usually occurs on the exposed surfaces. The rough periwinkle is one of the most misidentified species in the world. Throughout decades of searching the seashore, scientists and naturalists have named 113 different snail species and subspecies that later all proved to be rough periwinkles.

The distribution of the flat or blunt periwinkle (*Littorina obtusata*) is limited by its much smaller powers of resisting desiccation. It cannot survive on exposed surfaces when the tide is out, so it lives among the large seaweeds, especially bladder wrack (*Fucus vesiculosus*), which occurs in abundance on the mid-shore rocks.

ROUGH PERIWINKLE
Littorina saxatilis

SMALL PERIWINKLE
Melarhaphe neritoides

COMMON PERIWINKLE
Littorina littorea

FLAT PERIWINKLE
Littorina obtusata

FIG. 4: ALL SHOWN AT NATURAL SIZE

Hiding among the wet fronds of the seaweeds, it is kept moist and shaded from the sun when the tide is out. Its flat rounded shell resembles the bladders on the seaweed, sometimes making it difficult to find.

Although the common periwinkle (*Littorina littorea*) cannot live as high on the shore as the small and rough periwinkles, it is perhaps more perfectly adapted to shore life than the others, for it has a more extensive range. It not only occurs on the rocks from above mid-shore right down into the water below the lowest spring-tide level, but it is also quite happy on stones and mud, and can even survive on sand. It is, too, very tolerant to lowered salinity and flourishes in muddy estuaries. In fact some of the most flourishing winkle fisheries are situated in river estuaries.

By a special device, the common periwinkle is able to remain on an exposed rock surface unshaded from the sun. A layer of mucus is spread over the rock by the foot before it is withdrawn. The mouth of the shell is then cemented to the rock as the mucus dries, and loss of water is prevented. The adhesion is not very great, and a light tap, or even a gust of wind, can dislodge the winkle, which always sits with the spire of the shell downward. In any other position the shell is unbalanced and topples over as the mucus dries.

As with their powers to resist desiccation, so with their ability to breathe air, the four periwinkles form a graded series. The flat and common periwinkles both have a single ctenidium projecting into the mantle cavity, capable of extracting oxygen from air as well as from water, provided it is kept well moistened. Many shore animals have adapted their respiratory mechanisms in this way so that they can breathe alternately in air and water. As a consequence, complete immersion is for some of them as harmful as complete removal from the sea. Of the periwinkles, only the common winkle is capable of living wholly submerged in water.

The rough and small periwinkles have adapted themselves much more thoroughly than the other two species to air breathing. Their gills have become much reduced, so that they cannot endure immersion for long, while at the same time the wall of the mantle cavity has become richly supplied with blood-vessels, giving it the typical structure of a lung. By this means they are able to breathe in air for indefinite periods.

Small periwinkles have been known to survive without any sea water at all for several months. They are, in fact, in the adult stage, almost land animals. It is interesting to note that the lung cavity of land snails is developed from the mantle cavity of their aquatic ancestors, and it would seem that the small and rough periwinkles are gradually being modified so that they too, in time, may well be able to leave the shore altogether and take up a purely terrestrial existence. All through the ages the shore has been the most important habitat for animals changing from an aquatic to a terrestrial existence, so it is not surprising to find some present-day examples of this gradual movement away from the sea.

Although the rough periwinkle is not quite as able as the small periwinkle to resist desiccation and breathe indefinitely in air, it may be the first of the group to leave the shore altogether, because it has already made itself independent of the sea for reproduction. The fertilised eggs are retained within the body of the female, and are born as young snails complete with a tiny shell, and able to fend for themselves. Further development of the wall of the mantle cavity as a lung, and a somewhat greater capacity on the part of the tissues to resist evaporation of water, is all that is needed before the rough periwinkle is able to colonise the land.

The small periwinkle covers its eggs with an egg case after they have been internally fertilised, and liberates them into the sea during the winter months. An interesting adaptation to its position in the spring-tide splash zone is that reproductive activity occurs only once a fortnight, coinciding with the spring tides. At other times it would not be possible for the egg cases to be liberated into the water.

The little larvae which hatch out from the egg cases remain floating in the plankton for a considerable time. Many of them will of course provide food for various plankton-feeding animals. Those that survive will eventually settle down on the sea bed, many where conditions are unsuitable. Only those settling on weed-free rock on the mid-shore will be able to develop, and after a time they will crawl up the shore to make their permanent home in the splash zone. Drastic modification of the breeding methods of the small periwinkle is thus needed before it can completely emancipate itself from the water. The most it can achieve in the reasonably near future is an amphibian life, where the adult lives away from the shore but must return to the sea for the breeding season.

The larvae of the common periwinkle also have to face the hazards of a planktonic life. The female lays her eggs, usually one or two at a time, but occasionally three or four, in little helmet-shaped capsules. These are often liberated into the sea at flood tide and float away, or they are deposited on weeds. After hatching, the larvae drift about for some time before those that have survived settle and develop their shells.

Production of planktonic larvae is very wasteful, but it does enable the species to spread, and is a means of ensuring that all suitable areas are colonised. The flat periwinkle has sacrificed these advantages for greater protection of the young. Its egg cases are laid in masses among the fronds of the weeds on which it lives, and from them emerge tiny shelled young.

The behaviour patterns of the four periwinkle species are all different, each directing and confining the individuals of the species to that zone where conditions are most suitable to them.

The reactions of the winkles to gravity play a great part in zoning. They all show a negative response to the pull of gravity, causing them to move up the shore. This negative geotaxis is strongest in the small and rough periwinkles, taking them high up the shore and on to the exposed upper faces of the rocks. The common and flat periwinkles, in which this reaction is weaker, remain lower down the shore.

This reaction to gravity is tempered by the effects of desiccation and immersion, causing them to move down the shore if they are left uncovered by water for too long, and up the shore if immersed for too long. The common and rough periwinkles respond more strongly to the effects of desiccation than the other two species, which, however, are more sensitive to immersion. In this way each of the four species is confined to its optimum zone. If a mixed group of periwinkles is scattered at random on the shore, each will eventually move up or down the shore until it regains its own particular zone.

Their reactions to light do not carry them up or down the shore, but determine their position on the rocks within their zones. Small and rough periwinkles react fairly strongly towards light, and this carries them up to the exposed surfaces of the rocks, where they are found in greatest abundance. Reacting less strongly, the common periwinkle is found under rocks and in rock crevices as well as on the exposed surfaces, while the blunt periwinkle always moves away from the light, a reaction which carries it to the safety of the damp seaweeds and undersides of rocks.

Low temperatures are fatal to the common periwinkle, but its reactions enable it to escape from the effects of intense cold. When the temperature begins to approach a dangerous level, the winkle ceases to cling to the rocks and is swept down-shore by the tide until it reaches the safety of the water beyond the low-tide mark. On the return of warmer weather, its gravity reactions carry it back on to the shore.

The periwinkle fishery is not a very important branch of the British fishing industry judged on the national scale, yet locally it contributes to the economy of small fishing communities. Winkles can only be picked by hand and only at certain times of year in some parts of the country, according to various local regulations. In Sussex, winkle picking is allowed between May and September. The coastline between Beachy Head and Brighton provides seasonal income for many commercial winkle pickers. Some winkle fisheries have declined, including in estuaries in Kent and Essex, due to insufficient earnings to cover labour costs. Winkle prices are higher at Christmas when demand from France increases, so many fisheries only operate at this time.

Winkles dredged from the river channel are often covered with a spongy growth, and a tuft of carrageen moss (*Chondrus crispus*) is usually growing from the spire of the shell. Before the winkles can be marketed, these growths have to be removed.

When the dredges are hauled in, the winkles are sorted out from the mass of stones and empty shells of various sorts, and the tufts of carrageen moss nipped off with the thumb- and fingernails. At the end of the day the catch is washed overboard in a wire basket, the mesh being such that undersized winkles are returned to the water to continue their growth. Lastly, the winkles are stirred vigorously with sticks in pails of sea water, by which process the spongy growths are rubbed off.

The great difference between the various limpet shells we met in the previous chapter and periwinkle shells is that the former are not coiled, whereas the internal cavity of winkle shells, in common with most other gastropod shells, is rolled into a spiral. To fit into this spiral, the visceral mass of these animals is also coiled. Some shells are coiled one way, and others the opposite way. Dextral shells are those in which the shell whorls, followed from the apex to the aperture or opening of the shell, go in a clockwise direction, while sinistral shells show anti-clockwise coiling. The spiral line which follows the junction of the whorls is the suture. In some gastropods it lies in a pronounced groove, while in others it is only indicated by a very shallow depression.

Most gastropods normally have dextral shells, with sinistral shells occurring as rare freaks, but in a minority of species sinistral coiling is the rule, with dextral shells as occasional abnormalities. It is an interesting fact that during their early development limpets do pass through a stage when they have a minute coiled shell, the coiling disappearing as growth proceeds. This suggests that the limpets' ancestors probably had a coiled shell, the coiling having been subsequently lost.

The central axis around which the shell is coiled is known as the columella. This is sometimes hollow, the cavity or umbilicus opening close to the aperture of the shell. Presence or absence of an umbilicus is often a valuable aid in identifying gastropod species. A columella muscle running from the foot to the columella anchors the animal firmly to its shell. The rim of the shell aperture may be complete, or entire, or it may be interrupted by a groove known as the siphon groove. Its outer or free side is the outer lip, the inner lip being fixed to the lowest or body whorl of the shell. In some gastropods the margin of the lips is thickened to form a peristome.

With this information we can now look more closely at the shells of the four periwinkle species. They all have an entire aperture and a solid columella without an umbilicus. The shell whorls are close together so that in outline the shell is roughly cone-shaped with no deep groove following the suture. It is significant that most gastropods that live on rocks and are exposed to the full force of the waves and the tides have similar conical shells. Presumably this is an adaptation to their environment, reducing their resistance to water movement to a minimum. The smooth periwinkle has a blunt spire, but the other three species are pointed, the suture line of the rough periwinkle being a little more pronounced than that of the common periwinkle.

Attached to the upper surface of the hind part of the foot of every periwinkle is a roughly circular horny plate. This is the operculum. When the head and foot of the animal are withdrawn into the shell, it serves to close the shell aperture against intruders. All the periwinkles have a single pair of long tentacles, with an eye on a short stalk at the base of each. In the mantle cavity there is typically a single ctenidium.

Related to the periwinkles are the chink shells (*Lacuna* species). They are less well known than the periwinkles because they are confined mainly to the low-tide region and the shallow water beyond, where they live on the fronds of *Laminaria* and other tangleweeds. Their shells are thinner and more pointed than those of the periwinkle, but the most important difference is the presence of an umbilicus which is slit-shaped, and to which the name chink refers. Best known of the four species is the banded chink shell (*Lacuna vincta*), which has a beautiful, almost transparent shell banded in reddish brown on a white or yellowish ground. The bands are spiral and follow the shell whorls. Its eggs are laid in white rings on *Laminaria* and other fronds, and show up clearly against the dark background.

Of the eight British species of top shells, three are typically shore forms, while the other five really belong to the shallow water, extending from the low-water mark and occasionally being exposed at very low spring tides. Normally only their empty shells will be found cast up on the beach. The three shore species, like the common limpet, are characteristically animals of the rocks, and are never found on sand or mud. They may in fact be more closely related to the limpets than are the winkles. Better than any other coiled-shelled gastropods, their shells show secondary modification to a smooth cone by the almost complete elimination of the suture between the coils, representing an adaptation to their life exposed to the full force of the waves.

Zoning is very clearly shown by the three shore species. Highest on the shore is the thick top shell (*Phorcus lineatus*), which has a narrower zone than any other seashore animal, occupying a band often little more than a metre in width around the neap tide high-water mark. In this zone it sometimes occurs in great abundance. Its greyish shell is rather thick and unattractive, and up to 2.5 centimetres across. It is confined to the south and west coasts.

Occupying the widest zone is the flat top shell (*Steromphala umbilicalis*), which is about half the size of the thick top shell. On rocky shores it is found anywhere between low-water mark and neap tide high-water mark, where it overlaps the thick top shell zone. The shells of the two species cannot easily be confused, because apart from the difference in size the flat top shell is more delicately constructed and flatter, and its colour is light brown streaked with red.

THICK TOP SHELL
Phorcus lineatus

FLAT TOP SHELL
Steromphala umbilicalis

GREY TOP
SHELL
Steromphala cineraria

PAINTED TOP
SHELL
Calliostoma zizyphinum

PHEASANT SHELL
Tricolia pullus

WENTLETRAP
Epitonium clathrus

FIG. 5: PHEASANT SHELL: ×2 NATURAL SIZE;
OTHERS SHOWN AT NATURAL SIZE

Confined to the lower parts of the shore is the grey top shell or silver tommy (*Steromphala cineraria*), of similar size to the flat top shell but more pointed. Its colour is light grey streaked and spotted with purple-brown.

Of the shallow-water top shells the most common one is the painted top shell (*Calliostoma zizyphinum*), a very beautiful glossy shell of almost perfect cone shape about 2.5 centimetres across. Its colour varies from pale yellow to pink, with streaks of red.

The remainder of the group consists of four small shallow-water species averaging one centimetre across. Typically the top shells have an umbilicus, but in some it becomes covered by the shell aperture as the animal grows, and can only be distinguished when it is young. As with the winkles, there is always a horny operculum fixed to the upper surface of the hind part of the foot.

Top shells, like winkles, are vegetarians, feeding on seaweeds. With the exception of the painted top shell, their reproductive products are shed into the sea, and there is random fertilisation, as with limpets and chitons. From the eggs hatch planktonic larvae, which eventually change to small top shells and sink to the sea bed, with only those that fall on suitable rocky surfaces surviving. The painted top shell, however, lays its eggs in a long ribbon, and they are then fertilised. There is no planktonic stage, the eggs hatching direct to small top shells.

Quite closely related to the top shells is the pheasant shell (*Tricolia pullus*). Its semi-transparent glossy shell is conical, but the sutures are more clearly marked than in the top shells. Although only small, seldom exceeding a centimetre in length, it is a very beautiful shell. The ground colour is white or yellow, streaked and spotted with crimson or purple. There is no umbilicus. Pheasant shells are confined to the lower parts of the shore, and extend into shallow water. They are widely distributed, but most abundant on west and south-west coasts. In one respect the pheasant shell differs from top shells and winkles. Its operculum is not horny but calcareous.

So far in this and the previous chapter we have dealt with a number of very common and widely distributed groups of vegetarian snails and in the following chapter we shall consider the very important group of carnivorous snails. Before turning to these, however, we must look at a great variety of shells belonging to many different families. Most of them are small shells, often not very abundant or easy to find.

We begin, however, with one of our most attractive British shells, the wentletrap (*Epitonium clathrus*). The shell is in the form of a slender cone, up to four centimetres long and 1.5 centimetres wide at the aperture, consisting of fifteen or sixteen whorls separated by fairly deep sutures. Crossing the whorls are prominent ridges, a feature possessed by no other British shell.

The colour varies from cream to fawn, and there may be darker banding or mottling. A horny operculum closes the shell aperture, around which a prominent peristome is developed.

Living wentletraps can only be found at the extreme low-tide mark, for they are really shallow-water animals. If disturbed they are able to discharge a purple fluid into the water. As with so many other kinds of gastropods, larger and more beautiful species occur in tropical and subtropical seas. One large species known as the precious wentletrap, which occurs in eastern waters, was so sought after at one time that as much as £200 would be paid for a particularly fine shell.

The most exciting finds on the seashore are often achieved by searching the rocks and weeds at the extreme low-tide mark at spring tides, and in the shallow waters beyond. The weeds that grow here are particularly well worth examining, because all kinds of creatures can be found hidden away for protection among their fronds. Here with patience and care you may find several members of a family known as the spire shells (Rissoidae). They are all very tiny, averaging 2.5 millimetres or less in length, smaller that is than a full-grown small periwinkle. But many of them have most attractive shells. They are variously coloured, sometimes banded and mostly semi-transparent and glossy. Included in the family are members of two genera, *Rissoa* and *Cingula*.

Most of them have a high pointed shell. The majority of species are found all round our coasts, and several of them are abundant. If they were larger animals they would be much more familiar.

A somewhat larger species is the small needlewhelk (*Bittium reticulatum*), with its very slender shell about 1.5 centimetres long. It is similar in shape to the wentletrap, but smaller, and it also has fifteen or sixteen whorls, but the two can easily be distinguished because the needle-whelk has no prominent ridges running across the whorls of the shell.

The needlewhelk is one member of a small group of horn shells, represented by several genera. They are all, on the average, somewhat larger than the spire shells. Mention must be made of the reversed horn shell (*Monophorus perversus*), one of the minority of gastropods that normally has a sinistrally coiled shell. Full grown, its shell attains a length of about one centimetre.

Similar in shape and size to the horn shells is yet another group of shells found around the extreme low-water mark and beyond: the pyramid shells. The surface of those shells, however, is generally smooth, and the colour usually white.

3

The Carnivorous Snails

Of the dozen or so species of carnivorous snails found around our shores the most common and best known is the dog whelk (*Nucella lapillus*). It is found along with the limpets and common periwinkles on the weed-free rocks from mid-shore right down to low-water mark. In size it is similar to the common periwinkle, but in the colour and form of its shell it is quite distinctive. No other snail shows quite such a wide range of colouring. There are white, yellow, pink, pinkish-mauve and black ones, as well as individuals striped with two or more of these colours. A concentration of dog whelks showing these various colours can make quite an attractive display.

An examination of the dog whelk's shell shows two other features which distinguish it from any of the vegetarian snails we have previously dealt with. The shell wall is very much thicker, and the aperture is crossed at one point by a prominent groove, the siphon groove, a characteristic which the dog whelk shares with most other carnivorous snails. This siphon groove is connected with the creature's method of respiration. When the animal is covered with water a strip of mantle tissue coiled round to form a tube called the siphon passes out through this groove into the water. Through it a current of water is drawn into the mantle cavity and passes over the gill.

The siphon is really a device used by snails that live on sand or mud. By carrying the siphon in a vertical position

DOG WHELKS – *Nucella lapillus*

DOG WHELK
with siphon extended

DOG WHELK
ventral, showing
siphon groove

FIG. 6

its open end can be held well away from the mud or sand so that no particles get carried into the mantle cavity to clog it. The fact that the dog whelk possesses a siphon suggests that originally it lived on sand or mud, and only later changed its habits and became a rock snail.

The other great difference between the dog whelk and typical vegetarian snails lies in the structure and use of its radula. In vegetarian snails this is typically a wide band with a large number of teeth, and is capable of being protruded just beyond the mouth to enable the creature to scrape off its plant food. The dog-whelk radula on the other hand is much thinner, with fewer but more prominent teeth. It, too, is capable of being protruded as a proboscis a considerable way out of the mouth.

With this proboscis the dog whelk is able to sit on a limpet, top shell, periwinkle or mussel and bore a neat round hole in its shell. It is a laborious process, taking many hours, but when at last it is completed the proboscis is then thrust right through the hole, and the flesh of the victim methodically rasped away and carried back to its mouth as on a conveyor belt.

The little acorn barnacles which are so common on weed-free rocks are also a favourite item in the dog whelk's diet. With these, boring is unnecessary, for in some way not completely understood it is able to force apart the plates covering the barnacle and so reach its soft body.

Although capable of feeding on a variety of animals, the dog whelk is curiously conservative in its feeding habits, tending to confine itself to one kind of food so long as stocks last. If for example it is feeding on acorn barnacles, it will ignore completely the mussels which may be growing alongside and among them. Only when the supply of acorn barnacles in the immediate neighbourhood begins to fail will it turn its attention to the mussels, and will then ignore all barnacles until the supply of mussels begins to fail.

It is likely that the colour of a dog whelk's shell is genetically determined. Breeding studies of another, closely related species, the emarginate dog winkle (*Nucella emarginata*), show that colour, banding and spiral shell structure are inherited from one generation to the next. A study of dog whelks on the coast of Massachusetts found that on sheltered shores they were predominantly white, while on more exposed, wave-pounded shores the dog whelks were more variable in colour. Experiments showed that when brown dog whelks were moved to sheltered, sunny shores they heated up and desiccated faster compared to white shells in the same area. It could be that white shells are selected on sheltered shores because they reflect more heat and suffer less from desiccation compared to darker shells. Brown dog whelks living on a sheltered shore are likely to be more susceptible to overheating and may have to cut down the time they roam around hunting.

The reproductive products of the dog whelk are not shed into the sea. Breeding takes place in the early part of the year, the sexes mating before the female lays her eggs. These she produces in batches of several hundred, enclosing each batch in a small yellow egg capsule, about the size and shape of a grain of wheat. Laying the eggs and constructing the capsule takes about an hour, but each female may produce two dozen or more batches at one spawning, and in several successive spawnings she can produce up to three hundred capsules. The capsules are attached to the rocks, usually in a more or less upright position and sheltered in a shallow crevice or beneath an overhanging ledge.

Only about a dozen or so of the eggs in each capsule are fertilised. The remainder represent a store of food for the few that eventually hatch out after a development period of three or four months. These are very tiny but fully shelled individuals. When they crawl out of the top of the egg capsule they are carried down the shore by the receding tides until they are well below the zone occupied by the adults. For some time they feed mainly on the minute tube worms, *Spirorbis borealis*, which are very abundant in their tiny coiled tubes on the rocks near the low-tide mark. In this region they remain until they are about a centimetre long, when they migrate upshore into the adult zone.

Although it is now a very successful shore animal, the dog whelk does not seem to be in any way specially adapted to shore life. Its foot has no great adhesive power, though if it does get swept off the rocks by the waves its thick shell probably allows it to be rolled about without coming to any harm. Its rather thick tissues are probably fairly resistant to desiccation, because although it does possess an operculum, it seldom uses it to close its shell. Behind its head there is a small cavity containing a white fluid, which when exposed to the air changes through yellow and green to purple. It is easily fixed to a fast dye, and in earlier times was much used in Scotland and Ireland by the crofters to dye their homespun tweeds. The famous Tyrian purple of the Phoenicians is believed to have been obtained from a Mediterranean relative of the dog whelk, *Hexaplex trunculus*. Excavations along the Tyrian coast have revealed great piles of shells, often close to shallow depressions in the rocks which are thought to have been used as extracting pans.

Philip Henry Gosse recalls the legend of the discovery of the fabulous purple dye in the book *A Year at the Shore*.

The Tyrian Heracles was one day walking with his sweetheart along the shore, followed by her lap-dog, when the playful animal seized a shell that had just been washed up on the beach. Its lips were presently dyed with a gorgeous purple tint, which was traceable to a juice that was pressed out of the shellfish. The lady was charmed with the colour, and longed to have a dress of it; and, as wishes under such circumstances are laws, the enamoured hero set himself to gratify her, and soon succeeded in extracting and applying the dye, which afterwards became so famous.

In another book, *A Naturalist's Rambles on the Devonshire Coast*, Gosse describes experiments he carried out with the dye. On opening the dye cavity, he says:

you will find it filled with a substance exactly resembling in colour and consistence the pus or matter formed in a boil. You will not find much; that of a large Nucellus I managed to spread over a space of calico as large as a shilling. From its viscid consistence it is difficult to use with a pen, and I do not know how it may be uniformly diluted; but with a small camel's hair pencil I have used it with much more facility.

As soon as the matter is applied to the linen, its hue is a rich 'King's yellow', but becomes in a few minutes a delicate pea-green. In about an hour, if the weather be cloudy, it has become a yellow grass-green, from which it slowly and imperceptibly turns to a blue-green, thence to indigo, and thence to blue. A red tinge now becomes apparent, generally in parts, causing the hue to become first violet, then a purple more and more tinged with red, till at length, after five or six hours (in a room without direct sunlight) it assumes its final tint, a rather dull purplish crimson, or lake. The direct beams of the sun, however, greatly expedite the process, and at any stage will carry the remaining stages through to completion in a few minutes.

The dog whelk is a very widely distributed species, occurring all round the coast of western Europe from Portugal to the far north. It also occurs along the west coast of Iceland, and from Newfoundland down as far as New York.

Belonging to the same gastropod family (Muricidae) are two other British carnivorous snails, the sting winkle (*Ocenebra erinaceus*) and the oyster drill (*Urosalpinx cinerea*).

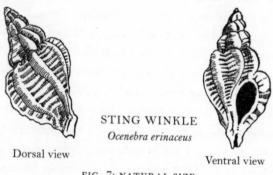

STING WINKLE
Ocenebra erinaceus

Dorsal view

Ventral view

FIG. 7: NATURAL SIZE

The whitish shell of the sting winkle is very distinctive with its prominent ribs, which give it a very 'spiky' appearance. Empty specimens washed in by the tide are often quite common among shingle. Like the dog whelk it has a prominent siphon groove and siphon, which it puts to good use, since it is found, typically, on stony and muddy ground from low-water mark to shallow water. The sting winkle is one of the principal enemies of the oyster, and a great pest on the oyster beds, boring through the oyster shells and devouring their contents with its long thin proboscis in the same way that the dog whelk destroys mussels. To the oyster fisherman the creature's proboscis is its 'sting', from which its name is derived. Like the dog whelk, it carries behind the head a small sac of liquid which turns purple on exposure to the air.

The third member of the family, the oyster drill, was not originally a British species but is now well established here. It was brought over accidentally, along with several other serious pests of the American oyster beds, during the various unsuccessful attempts to supplant the dwindling stocks of native English oysters with American ones. Although the oysters themselves failed to survive for any length of time, these pests have thrived and spread, transferring their attentions to native English oysters with serious consequences. The oyster drills' methods of dealing with their prey are precisely similar to those adopted by the sting winkles and dog whelks, shells being bored and the contents extracted by a long thin proboscis. They show a preference for young oysters in their first year, and have been calculated to eat as many as forty in twelve months.

So hardy is the oyster drill that it can withstand very cold weather better than our native dog whelks and sting winkles. In the exceptionally cold winter of 1928–29 the Essex oyster beds were practically cleared of these latter species, but the oyster drills were unaffected. During the few succeeding years they were able to increase rapidly as they had very little competition to contend with.

Like the dog whelk and sting winkle, the oyster drill, or whelk tingle as it is sometimes called, does not spawn into the water but lays its eggs in capsules which it usually attaches to oyster shells. In consequence, its ability to migrate is fortunately fairly limited.

Another rather unusual gastropod introduced from America, probably at about the same time as the oyster drill, is the slipper limpet (*Crepidula fornicata*). Although superficially it looks somewhat like a flattened limpet, it is not really related to the limpets, but is a distant relative of the periwinkles. Its shell has a curious internal ledge, so that looked at from beneath it does appear something like a slipper.

 Dorsal  Ventral

SLIPPER LIMPET – *Crepidula fornicata*

FIG. 8

Its method of feeding is quite unlike that of any other gastropod. It makes no use of a radula, but instead it has much enlarged gills which trap minute food particles that come in suspended in the respiratory current of water, a method of feeding which we shall find is typical of the bivalve molluscs. Although therefore quite incapable of attacking the oysters or of harming them directly in any way, it often overlies them on the oyster beds in such numbers as to smother them. Also, by filtering out the food particles from the water before it gets down to the oysters, it deprives them of much of their food.

Again, unlike typical gastropods but like many bivalves, it is a sedentary creature which does not move about. Instead it has an unusual habit of living in piles, one animal sitting on the back of another until a more or less permanent chain of as many as nine individuals is formed, the lowest animals being the oldest. These are always females, while the top two or three, the youngest in the chain, are males. Those in between are intermediate, in the process of changing from male to female.

When and where the slipper limpet was first introduced into this country is not known, but it was first recorded here in the 1880s. Since then the first introductions have probably been reinforced several times along with successive introductions of the American oyster. Today it is found all around our coasts from the Humber down to Devon. In the inter-war years it appeared on the coast of Holland, having probably travelled attached to floating driftwood or seaweed. It then proceeded to spread to the shores of Germany and Denmark.

On muddy or sandy shores from the low-tide mark into shallow water there lives a distinctive carnivorous snail, the netted dog whelk (*Tritia reticulata*), complete with long siphon and siphon groove. The shell itself is often half buried in the sand and mud over which the creature walks, and is coloured and sculptured to blend with its surroundings. The ground colour is yellow dotted with white and brown, and the surface is broken up by horizontal and vertical ribbing to give it a very rough appearance. The sutures between the whorls are well marked, and the general shape is that of a narrow cone up to about three centimetres high and two centimetres across at the aperture. A smaller species, the thick-lipped dog whelk (*Tritia incrassata*), is found on rocky ground at low-tide mark and beyond.

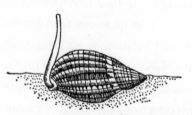 

Buried in sand   Ventral

NETTED DOG WHELK – *Tritia reticulata*

FIG. 9

Although some of the carnivorous snails already dealt with in this chapter are able, by virtue of their long siphons, to live on soft sand or mud, and even sink their bodies partially into it, they are not able actually to burrow into it. There are, however, two species of carnivorous snails that not only live buried completely in sand but rely for their food on other sand-burrowing molluscs. These are the necklace shell (*Euspira catena*) and the pale moon snail (*Euspira pallida*).

To enable them to plough their way through the sand, their foot is much enlarged and very powerful. Living in the sand are also various species of bivalve molluscs which we shall meet in a later chapter. The snails work their way through the upper layers of the sand in search of these bivalves, and when they find one they attack it using the same method employed by other carnivorous snails. They bore a hole in their victim's shell and then proceed to rasp out its body at leisure. In their drilling operations they are aided by a gland on the under-surface of the proboscis. This secretes acid which dissolves the shell. You may well find a bivalve shell that has been bored through by *Natica*. *Natica* shells can generally only be found by digging. They are easily recognisable because they are very smooth and rounded to facilitate their movement through the sand.

The largest of all our gastropod molluscs, and one of the best known because it is the only one besides the periwinkle that is eaten in any numbers, is the common whelk (*Buccinum undatum*), whose thick dull whitish shell attains a length of ten centimetres and a breadth of six centimetres. It is a widely distributed carnivorous snail extending from the low-tide mark into quite deep water. There is a wide siphon groove and a long siphon which can be carried well above the sea bed, and a long and powerful proboscis.

Full-grown whelks are never found on the shore, only the empty shells after their occupants have died, but smaller specimens may sometimes be found sheltering on stretches of mud between rocks. The whelk's diet is varied. It will eat all kinds of dead molluscs as well as living ones. In tackling living oysters and other bivalves it shows considerable ingenuity, waiting on top of the

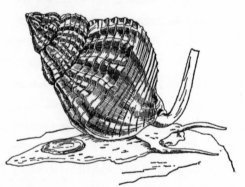 

COMMON WHELK – *Buccinum undatum*
with siphon extended

COMMON WHELK
showing siphon groove

FIG. 10

oyster's shell until the oyster raises its upper valve, at which point the snail turns quickly round on its foot and inserts the edge of its own shell between the valves, thus holding them sufficiently apart to enable the proboscis to reach and devour the soft body within. Whelks are also said sometimes to grip small bivalves with their feet and force the edges together until small pieces are broken off. The proboscis can then be inserted through the small openings that are made.

The flesh of the whelk is very tough and requires prolonged boiling before it can be eaten. Nevertheless, it is a very popular shellfish, sharing a stall with the bivalve cockle at many a seaside town. Whelks are caught mainly in in-shore waters by small boats using baited pots which are lowered onto the sea bed and marked with floating buoys. The designs vary, but they can be circular plastic or metal pots with a funnel-shaped mouth through which whelks crawl to get to the bait. When the pots are hauled back up to the surface, the whelks are still alive inside.

Whelks lay their eggs in large capsules, many being fastened together and anchored to rocks or to the sea bed. After the young have hatched and crawled out of the capsules, the whole mass of empty capsules, sometimes as large as a football and having a similar appearance and texture to a sponge, is washed up on the shore, where it is a familiar object among the flotsam.

One of the most beautiful and delicate of all our gastropods, and one that is quite unlike all the others is the cowrie (*Trivia monacha*). The adult shell, seldom much more than six millimetres long, is roughly oval in shape and crossed by two dozen or so delicate ribs. It shows no signs of coiling, but young specimens have tiny coiled shells. As they grow, however, the outer whorl grows over the inner ones to hide them. The aperture, too, is unusual, being elongated and slit-like, instead of rounded as in all other British gastropods.

COWRIE
Trivia monacha

Ventral

FIG. 11: ×2 NATURAL SIZE

Nearly all snail shells go on growing throughout the life of their occupants, but once the cowrie shell has achieved its adult form it never increases in size. Another unusual feature of the cowrie is that when it walks, not only the head and foot but most of the mantle is protruded from the shell, the mantle folds being turned upwards to cover and meet over the top of the shell. The protection which these mantle folds give to the shell explains why it retains its high gloss throughout life.

Despite their small size, the cowries are carnivorous

in their feeding habits, their food consisting of the minute individuals of compound sea-squirt colonies, which they are able to extract from the jelly in which they are embedded by means of a long radula protruded from the end of a slender proboscis.

Cowries lay their eggs in tiny mushroom-shaped capsules, which are usually planted with their stalks embedded in the jelly of a sea-squirt colony. From the eggs in these capsules hatch tiny larvae, which escape and live a drifting planktonic life before changing to young cowries and settling down on the sea bed.

Although our own cowries are so small, many tropical species grow to a large size and possess some of the most beautiful of all mollusc shells.

Another group of carnivorous snails which live from the low-tide mark into shallow water are the Turridae or conelets, so named from their slender cone-shaped shells, which are of general whelk shape but seldom attain three centimetres in length.

The Velutinidae are distinguished from other families by the fact that their shells are internal, being permanently covered by the extensive mantle and not temporarily covered as in the cowries. The velvet shell is oval in shape, semi-transparent, and with a very wide aperture. There are three common species, each rather more than 1.5 centimetres long when full-grown, and they all feed on various kinds of sea-squirts.

Velvet shells are found under stones on the lower part of the shore, and also extend beyond the low-tide mark. The permanent overgrowth of the shell by the mantle is unusual for the subclass Caenogastropoda, but it is much more common in another branch of the gastropods, the Heterobranchia, which we shall consider in the following chapter.

4

Bubble Shells, Sea-Slugs
and Tusk Shells

All the various gastropod shells that we have so far considered belong to the subclasses Patellogastropoda, Vetigastropoda and Caenogastropoda. It is now time to turn our attention to the members of the subclass Heterobranchia, in which full torsion has been to varying degrees reversed. The heterobranchs are typically hermaphrodites, with male and female reproductive organs in each individual.

Members of this subclass are divided into numerous orders, including the Cephalaspidae and the Nudibranchia. In the former group the shell is often much reduced and is sometimes completely covered by extensive folds of the mantles, as it is in the cowries. In the nudibranchs, however, the shell has become completely suppressed in the adults. In the younger stages there is a shell, but this is shed either before the eggs hatch or in the larval stage. The word nudibranch comes from Greek and Latin words meaning naked gills. They breathe through external gills; in some nudibranchs the gills are a ring of feathery plumes surrounding the anus; some have numerous finger-like projections called cerata along their backs which act as gills and make nudibranchs look like they are covered with coarse fur or wool. At the front end, club-shaped tentacles called rhinophores detect chemical odours in the water (these can look rather like ears and lead to the common name for some nudibranchs of 'sea bunnies').

Bubble shell is the common name for assorted heterobranchs that have very delicate shells. *Acteon tornatalis* is smooth, reddish in colour, oval in shape and sharply pointed. With its seven whorls it is still unmistakably a snail shell. Acteon shells are found mainly on sandy coasts, the animals living from the extreme low-water mark into shallow water. The shell is large enough to contain the whole animal, and there is a horny operculum to close the rather elongated aperture. The tentacles are broad and flattened, and carried erect over the front part of the shell. There is a well-developed mantle cavity and a single ctenidium.

Other heterobranchs show increasing divergence from a typical snail form. There are some half dozen species of bubble shell occurring in Britain that show reduction in the shell. Their shells are cylindrical and look something like normal coiled shells with all but the top part cut off. There is no longer room for the whole body, which cannot therefore be completely retracted, and there is consequently no operculum. Lateral extensions of the large foot are used for swimming, and when not required are folded against the shell, partially covering it.

The most common bubble shells are the blunt bubble shells (*Retusa obtusa*) found mainly from low-water mark in muddy or sandy estuaries; *Haminoea hydatis* and *Haminoea elegans*, found on muddy shores; and the soft bubble shell, *Akera bullata*, also an inhabitant of shore mud. Its glossy greenish shell is semi-transparent and elastic.

BLUNT BUBBLE SHELL
Retusa obtusa

FIG. 12: ×4 NATURAL SIZE

The next stage in shell reduction is represented by the lobe shell (*Philine aperta*). Externally there is no trace of the very thin shell, which is covered from the front by a shield formed from the broad flattened tentacles, at the sides by lateral extensions of the foot, and from behind by an upturned mantle lobe.

Reduction of the shell, which is flat and completely covered by the mantle, and development of lateral lobes of the foot as swimming organs is carried still further in the largest, the best known and the most fascinating of all our heterobranchs, the sea-hare (*Aplysia punctata*).

The name derives from one of its two pairs of tentacles, which are flattened and held vertically like a pair of broad ears. Its olive-green body may be as much as ten centimetres long. Young specimens, whose colour is reddish brown to match the red seaweeds on which they feed, live in shallow water beyond the tide mark, only coming on shore as they approach full size, when they change their colour and their feeding habits, henceforward confining themselves exclusively to the green seaweed known as sea-lettuce.

That a creature of such weird appearance should have given rise to sinister beliefs concerning it is not surprising. Gosse remarked that the sea-hare

has a mythic history full of wild romance. Our species has been often called *depilans*, because the fluid which exudes from it was said to have the power of causing the hair to fall from the human head which it touched; and the common species of Southern Europe retains the appellation in the records of science. The Mediterranean fishermen have so great a horror of it that no bribes will induce them to handle it willingly; and they tell strange stories of wounds being produced, limbs being mortified, and even death itself being caused by accidental or foolhardy contact with the patent creature.

Darwin recorded that a species of sea-hare which he found in the Cape Verde islands produced a secretion spread over its body which caused a sharp stinging sensation similar to that produced by the Portuguese man-of-war.

Gosse also refers to the sinister employment of the sea-hare by the Romans.

In those dark days of the Empire when no one's life was secure against insidious assassination, and when professed poisoners were at the command of such as could afford to pay their hire, this mollusc was an essential element of the fatal draught. Locusta used it to destroy such as were inimical to Nero; it entered into the potion which she prepared for the tyrant himself; and Domitian was accused of having given it to his brother Titus. To search after the sea-hare was to render one's self suspected; and when Apuleius was accused of magic because he had induced a rich widow to marry him, the principal proof against him was that he had hired the fishermen to procure him this fearful animal. He succeeded, however, in showing, to the satisfaction of his judges, that his object was merely the gratification of laudable scientific curiosity.

Setting aside the magical and mythical stories about sea-hares, these gastropods do in fact produce a remarkable chemical in the clouds of crimson ink they release when disturbed by predators. A close relative from North America, *Aplysia californica*, secretes a chemical known as escapin, which deters predators, in particular spiny lobsters. While giving the sea-hare time to escape from attackers, escapin also has antimicrobial properties and sea-hares may use it to protect their eggs.

Another of the heterobranch molluscs is one called *Pleurobranchus membranaceus*, which is really a shallow-water species that comes onto the lower parts of the shore during the summer months in order to feed on the sea-squirts that live under stones and in rock pools. Its shell has become reduced to a thin flat plate completely covered by extensive folds of the mantle.

Although they have completely lost their shells, this account of seashore molluscs would be incomplete without some reference to the Nudibranchia, the nudi-branchs. Not only have they lost their shells, but with it both the mantle cavity and the ctenidium have dis-appeared. Secondary gills have developed that take over the function of breathing.

These naked snails, or sea-slugs as they are often called, though they are not closely related to the familiar land slugs, are among the most beautiful of all the mol-luscs. They are variously and often brightly coloured, with all manner of feathery outgrowths functioning as gills. Only when seen alive and in water, when these delicate outgrowths are properly displayed, can the full beauty of these sea-slugs be appreciated.

A relatively common nudibranch on British shores is the sea-lemon (*Doris pseudoargus*), whose yellowish body mottled with specks of green, red or purple attains a length of eight centimetres when full grown. It feeds on the yellowish crumbs-of-bread sponge, against which it is extremely difficult to detect. The sea-lemon produces a very characteristic spawn in the form of a white gelatinous coiled ribbon about 2.5 centimetres in width and up to twenty-five centimetres long. As it is laid, one edge is glued to the rock. A single ribbon has been calculated to contain as many as fifty thousand developing eggs, each of which eventually hatches to a minute planktonic larva.

Another common British nudibranch is the type with furry-looking cerata along its back. This is the grey sea-slug (*Aeolidia papillosa*), which is of similar size to the sea-lemon. It is found under stones in rock pools on the lower parts of the shore. The cerata are numerous and look something like a thick mat. Each is hollow, the cavity representing an offshoot from the digestive system with a most unusual function. All the sea-slugs of this second group feed on sea-anemones and other coelenterates, all of which contain sting or nettle cells on their tentacles. These are not destroyed as they pass through the sea-slug's gut, but in some way are diverted into the cerata, where they accumulate near the top. Presumably they help to protect the sea-slugs from fish which would otherwise eat them, in the same way that they protected their original owners.

A third type of sea-slug is much less common on the shore than the other two. One of the largest, the bushy-backed slug (*Dendronosus frondosus*), although really a shallow-water species, does sometimes turn up in rock pools near the low-tide mark. Its numerous much-branched lateral processes give it a very feathery appearance, and its colour, best described as red marbled with brown and spotted with white and yellow, makes it very difficult to detect among the seaweed fronds on which it lives and feeds.

To complete our studies of marine single-shelled molluscs, we must now look at an unusual shell that is often cast up empty on the shore. This is the elephant's tusk shell (*Antalis entalis*) which, like the coat-of-mail shells, represents a distinct but small class.

ELEPHANT'S TUSK SHELL
Antalis entalis

FIG. 13: NATURAL SIZE

The name derives from the fact that the white shell does resemble a miniature elephant's tusk, between 2.5 and five centimetres long, in which the tip has been cut off so that it is open at both ends. During life, the tusk shell lies buried in the sand below the extreme low-tide mark, with the narrow end of the shell projecting just above the surface. Through this opening a respiratory current of water is drawn over the mantle, which has taken over the functions of the gills, these having disappeared. The mantle is in the form of a tube lining the tubular shell, which in the larva is formed as two separate halves which subsequently fuse to a single tube. To move through the sand the tusk shell projects its foot through the lower aperture.

Compared with any gastropod, the head of *Antalis* is much reduced, and has neither tentacles nor eyes. The mouth, however, is surrounded by slender filaments which catch the minute living creatures on which the tusk shell feeds. Tusk shells are more common in the north than in the south. Besides the elephant's tusk shell there is also a smaller species having a similar distribution. This is the grooved-tusk shell (*Antalis vulgata*), which is creamy rather than white in colour. It is more sharply curved than its larger relative, and shows distinct longitudinal grooving.

We have now followed the complete history of the marine gastropod shell from the simple uncoiled condition of the limpets through all kinds of coiled variations, and now in this chapter we have traced its gradual reduction and disappearance.

5

Mussels and the Bivalve Pattern

The common mussel (*Mytilus edulis*) is the obvious choice to introduce the bivalve molluscs (known in the past as Lamellibranchs). It is by far the most common of all the seashore bivalves; few other animals are as well adapted in structure and function to shore life. Although there are sufficient similarities between the bivalves and gastropods to make it clear that both share the same fundamental structure, there are also several profound differences.

The shell of the mussel consists of two halves or valves, hinged along one edge and enclosing a body showing similar bilateral symmetry. In many species each valve possesses projecting teeth called hinge teeth which fit into corresponding pits in the opposite valve. Covering the body is an extensive mantle consisting of separate right and left halves draped over the body like two curtains. Each lines one of the shell valves, and is responsible both for its initial formation and its subsequent growth. The first part of the shell to be laid down is the umbo, which is that part of the shell recognisable as a hump or break near the top edge. Lines of growth running parallel with the edge of the umbo are usually well marked.

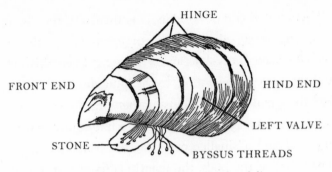

COMMON MUSSEL – *Mytilus edulis*

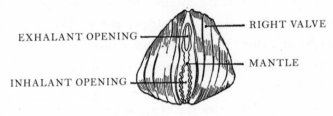

COMMON MUSSEL from behind

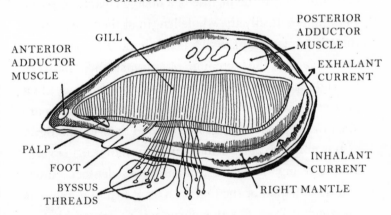

COMMON MUSSEL with left valve and mantle removed

FIG. 14: ×1.5 NATURAL SIZE

The pointed end of the mussel is the front, the hinge, consisting of an elastic ligament arranged so that it tends to keep the valves open, running from this end over the back of the animal to the hind end. Connecting the valves, and capable of closing them tightly when they contract, are two adductor muscles, a larger one near the hind end and a smaller one near the front. Along the upper part of the body the mantle is fixed to the body, but below it hangs free as two continuous curtains one on each side of the body, the free edges being frilled. At the hind end the right and left mantles are partially united, leaving two openings one above the other.

If the two adductor muscles are cut and one of the shell valves removed, the body of the mussel can be examined by turning back the exposed mantle. Immediately internal to the mantle is a double curtain of tissue running practically the whole length of the body. This is the gill or ctenidium, which is much more elaborate and extensive than the ctenidium of any gastropod. Between the right and left ctenidia a conical-shaped muscular foot projects downwards and forwards. When the valves are open the foot can be projected beyond their lower edges.

It is not, however, normally used for movement, except in very young mussels. The mussel is a sedentary animal, and the function of the foot is to fix it firmly to the rock on which it lives. For this purpose it possesses a byssus gland producing a sticky liquid which when discharged runs down a groove towards its tip. This is placed on the rock and at once withdrawn, leaving a thread which hardens rapidly. By repeating the process a whole series of such byssus threads can be produced, having sufficient strength to enable the animal to maintain its hold even in the roughest seas. So strong is the byssus that it is quite difficult to pull a mussel off the rock to which it is anchored. The byssus gland is believed to be a modification of the gland in the snail's foot that produces the slime on which it walks.

A common feature of sedentary marine animals is loss of sense organs and reduction or disappearance of the head. A creature unable to move about either in search of food or to avoid its enemies has little need of elaborate sense organs. So we find that in contrast with the well-developed head of the gastropods the mussel is practically headless. There are no tentacles or sense organs, only a mouth surrounded by two flaps of tissue called palps, whose function is to sort out the food before it passes into the mouth. The only sense organs it possesses are a series of small sensory tentacles on the hind edge of the mantle surrounding the lower of the two openings.

When the tide is out mussels are inactive and their valves closed tightly. Only when the sea returns to cover them do they relax their adductor muscles and allow the elastic ligaments to open their shells. A continuous current of water is then drawn in through the lower opening left by the mantle flaps at the hind end of the body. This water passes through numerous minute channels which perforate the gills, finally passing out again through the upper mantle opening. These two openings are known as the inhalant and exhalant siphons. The sensory tentacles surrounding the inhalant siphon serve to test the water as it enters.

The respiratory current of water is caused by the rhythmic beating of myriads of minute hair-like cilia which cover the surface of the gills. Besides providing the mussel with the oxygen it needs, this current of water also brings in its food. The gill perforations are so small that even microscopic diatoms cannot pass through them. These and other small plankton organisms are trapped on the surface, where they are taken up by a sticky mucus produced by certain of the surface cells. Other cilia convey this mucus with its trapped food particles towards the mouth, where the palps sort them out, only allowing diatoms and particles of similar size to enter the mouth. Any larger particles are rejected and leave the mussel by the exhalant stream, along with the undigested remains of the food after it has passed through the gut.

This method of extracting plankton suspended in the water is known as suspension feeding, and is adopted by many bivalves and other marine animals. The advantages of the method, with each tide bringing abundant fresh supplies of food, are considerable, and make it possible for great concentrations of mussels, oysters and other bivalves to live and thrive packed closely together. The amount of water filtered by a heavy population must be very great, since each individual filters many litres of water at each tide. Experiments on an American species showed that about two litres of water entered the inhalant siphon and passed through the gills every hour. The efficiency of suspension feeding is shown by figures for total growth rate on a flourishing mussel bed. In a year this can amount to as much as 45,000 kilograms to the hectare, including 11,000 kilograms of actual mussel meat. In contrast, good pasture can produce between 100 and 200 kilograms of beef per hectare in a year.

Spawning takes place in the spring, the reproductive products being shed into the mantle cavity and passing out with the exhalant current. The trigger which sets off spawning is the temperature of the water. When this reaches a certain minimum figure a few individuals begin to spawn, and the presence of their reproductive products in the water in some way stimulates all the other individuals in the same area to spawn, so that within a short time the whole bed is actively spawning. Such a mechanism of mutual stimulation is an obvious advantage where random fertilisation without mating has to be relied on, because it produces maximum concentration of reproductive products in the water, and therefore ensures a high proportion of fertilised eggs. As with so many other marine animals, the eggs hatch to planktonic larvae, which can be widely distributed before they settle. When a larva does finally settle it can move about on its foot for a time while searching for a suitable spot to fix its byssus threads.

Mussels are not only among the most abundant and successful of all seashore animals, they also have one of the widest zones, being able to flourish anywhere from well up the shore into shallow offshore water. They are able to fix themselves to stones buried in shallow mud as well as to exposed rocks and stones. On a muddy shore or estuary the byssus threads are formed longer than usual to allow the animal itself to be above the surface of the mud and so be able to draw in a clean current of water. Despite the firmness with which a mussel is fixed by its byssus threads, it can if the necessity arises break them and travel to a new site, where a fresh byssus is produced.

Mussels are extremely prolific, almost every available rock space being covered with large and small specimens. A striking example of their reproductive and colonising efficiency occurred in Holland towards the end of the Second World War. When the Germans blew up the Walcheren dykes in 1944 the land behind them was flooded with sea water. The following year, the dykes were repaired and the water pumped away. During the time that they had been covered with water, mussel larvae had settled on the walls of houses, on fences and even on trees, and these were found to be covered with growing mussels as the water was removed.

Economically, the mussel is second only among molluscs to the oyster. Large quantities are used both for bait and for food. In Scotland huge quantities were once gathered to bait the long lines that were in common use by the fishing fleets. To collect the mussels and bait the thousands of hooks carried on these lines was the job of the fishermen's wives and daughters. Less long-line fishing is now done, having been largely replaced by other methods, so there has been a substantial reduction in mussel gathering for bait.

Flourishing natural mussel beds are sufficiently common in Britain to make artificial cultivation unnecessary. In France, however, mussel cultivation has gone on for centuries. The method used is said to have been discovered by an Irish sailor who was shipwrecked on a lonely part of the west coast of France in 1235. In order to feed himself he made crude nets of grass and attached these to stakes driven into the mud well down the shore when the tide was out, the idea being that fish would become trapped in these nets as the tide came in, and could be gathered after it had gone out again.

Whether he had much success in catching fish we do not know. He did, however, make the important discovery that mussel larvae settled on the nets, which soon became covered with developing mussels. A similar method is still being used in France to cultivate mussels, with twigs in place of grass to provide the necessary surface on which the mussel larvae can settle.

The greatest problem connected with the use of mussels as food is bacterial contamination. Many of the best mussel beds occur where there is a danger that the water covering them has become contaminated by sewage discharged into the sea. These bacteria will pass into the mussels with the inhalant current and may become trapped by the gills. Such mussels are unfit for human consumption because they may spread bacterial diseases if they are eaten.

One of the most extensive of all British mussel beds occurs at Conwy in North Wales, and has always been a principal source of mussels for food. In 1912 the sale of mussels from these beds was prohibited because it was found that many of them were being contaminated with sewage bacteria. This led to investigations to find means of purifying contaminated mussels so as to make them safe for human consumption. The remedy proved a simple one. It was found that if the mussels were removed from the natural beds and put into clean sea water for a day they cleared themselves of all bacteria. As a result, tanks for mussel purification were erected wherever substantial quantities of mussels were collected for food. After purification they are packed into sterilised bags which are sealed before being sent to market.

Being filter feeders, mussels are one of the aquatic animals that absorb minute particles of plastic debris from the water. These small fragments, known as microplastics and under five millimetres in size, come from various human sources, including larger pieces of plastic debris that break down, plastic beads added to cosmetics and cleaning products, and synthetic fibres from clothes, fishing ropes and nets. A 2018 study found that mussels from the wild and on sale in supermarkets were widely contaminated with microplastics. It is not yet known what impact microplastics have on the mussels themselves or their ecosystems, and it remains uncertain whether microplastics in food, such as mussels, causes any health problems for people.

Despite their great abundance, mussels are not without their enemies. The dog whelk, as we have already seen, takes its toll of those that grow on the shore. In the sea the principal enemy is the starfish, which, although lacking jaws, teeth or any other form of offensive weapon, is nevertheless able to open and consume mussels. Small specimens are grasped by the numerous adhesive tube feet, which run in two rows all along the under-surface of the five arms, and are pushed through the mouth into the stomach. Here the contents are digested and the empty shell eventually ejected.

The method adopted with larger specimens is more remarkable. The starfish hunches its body over the mussel, grips the two valves of the shell with its tube feet, and pulls steadily. Its muscles are not as powerful as the adductor muscles of its potential victim, but they have greater powers of endurance. After an hour or so the mussel begins to tire and then, slowly, the starfish is able to draw the valves apart. It has, however, no means of extracting the soft body from its shell. Instead, it everts its stomach through its mouth and wraps it round the mussel, pouring digestive juices over it. The products of digestion are absorbed through the stomach wall in the normal way. When the meal is over, the stomach is withdrawn again through the mouth.

Curious little pea crabs are sometimes found living in mussels, where they are protected from their enemies. They do little damage beyond diverting some of the mussels' food to their own use, and perhaps occasionally nibbling little pieces of mantle. As the female pea crab grows, it often becomes too big to leave its host's body, so must spend the rest of its life imprisoned there. The males, however, are smaller, and can continue to travel in and out of their hosts' bodies at will, which they do during the breeding season, moving from shell to shell in search of the females.

Besides the common mussel there are several other British marine mussels. Larger than the common mussel is the horse mussel (*Modiolus modiolus*), whose shell is similar, but the pointed beak is not quite at the front end of each valve, as it is in the common species. It is a shallow-water animal, which burrows into muddy gravel. With the aid of byssus threads it binds a number of stones together to form a kind of nest in which it lies. It is more common in the north than the south. Full-grown specimens average about thirteen centimetres in length, but occasional individuals up to twenty-three centimetres long are found. Unlike its smaller relative, its flesh is too coarse to eat.

The bearded horse mussel (*Modiolus barbatus*) and the bean horse mussel (*Modiolula phaseolina*) are much smaller species, attaining a maximum length of 2.5 centimetres. Both are shallow-water species with habits similar to those of the horse mussel. They are, however, distinguished from all other mussels by the fact that the outer horny layer of the shell is prolonged in the form of a fringe of thorn-like projections – the 'beard'. The shell of the bearded horse mussel is orange or scarlet, but the colour is partially masked by the yellowish-brown horny layer. The colour of the bean horse mussel is yellowish tinged with purple. Complete specimens of any of the horse mussels are unlikely to be found on shore, only empty shells being washed in by the tide.

Largest of all the British bivalve molluscs is the fan mussel (*Atrina fragilis*). The shell has the form of an elongated triangle, more than twice as long as it is broad at its wider end, and often thirty centimetres or more in length. It is found in shallow water just beyond the extreme low-tide mark, usually lying partially buried in an upright position in mud or fine gravel, firmly

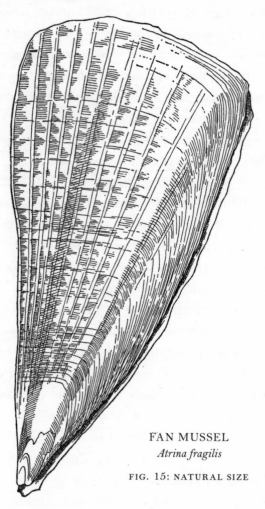

FAN MUSSEL
Atrina fragilis

FIG. 15: NATURAL SIZE

anchored to stones well beneath the surface by a long and very strong byssus. The wide hind end projects several centimetres above the surface so that an inhalant current free from mud or sand can be drawn in. Fan mussel shells are horn-coloured, thin and brittle, and at the hind end do not close completely even when the adductor muscles are fully contracted. The fan mussel is one of Britain's rarest and most threatened mollusc species. Damage caused by fishing trawlers and dredgers is a major threat to their survival. They are a protected species in Britain and it is illegal to deliberately injure or kill them, possess or sell them.

A close relative of the fan mussel is the noble pen shell, *Pinna nobilis*, from the Mediterranean. Stories tell of their silky, golden byssus threads being used for thousands of years to weave into a fine material called sea silk. It is said that Roman emperors wore garments made from sea silk, and ancient Egyptian mummies were wrapped in this cloth. There were tales of aquatic sheep living underwater and occasionally coming to shore to scratch themselves on rocks, leaving behind clumps of their golden fleece. In fact, these ancient materials were probably other fine cloths, made of cotton or linen, and a mistake in translating the word byssus from Greek led to the enduring myths about sea silk. Nevertheless, there has been a small-scale industry making genuine sea silk from the byssus threads of noble pen shells, based mainly in southern Italy and on the island of Sardinia. The oldest surviving piece of genuine sea silk dates back to the fourteenth century, a knitted cap found in Paris. Today, the processing and weaving of byssus threads into sea silk is a dying tradition practised by only a handful of people. Also, like fan mussels, noble pen shells are threatened with extinction and collecting them alive is illegal.

The shape of these various mussel shells is not typical of bivalves as a whole. That part of the shell behind the umbo has been enlarged, and the part in front of it much reduced. The shell is described as inequilateral, to distinguish it from the more common type of equilateral shell in which the parts behind and in front of the umbo are equally developed. Both valves are, however, similar in shape and size, the shell being described as equivalve, to distinguish it from inequivalve shells in which one valve is larger than the other or of different shape from it.

It has been suggested that the unusual proportions of the mussel shell are an adaptation to its life exposed to the waves. The byssus is directed forward so that the shell will tend to swivel round like a weather vane, the narrow front end facing the flow of the water and consequently offering minimum resistance to it. Where they are growing close together, though, the mussels cannot move, but they then protect each other from the full force of the moving water.

Among the shells that rely upon byssus threads for

anchorage there is one that has an equilateral shell, the ark shell (*Arca tetragona*). It is rather an angular shell, yellow to reddish brown in colour and up to four centimetres long, and the umbos or beaks of the two valves are widely separated, not close together as they are in the mussels. Ark shells are found only on the lower parts of the shore, where they hide away in crevices and under ledges, attaching themselves by their byssus threads to rocks or to other bivalve shells.

Although primarily interested in the shells of the seashore, you might well stray to the neighbouring rivers and ponds, and here you would find several freshwater relatives of the marine mussels. In ponds and lakes lives one of the most common and largest of them, the swan mussel (*Anodonta cygnea*), which often occurs in large colonies. Its shell is more oval than that of the common mussel, and greenish yellow in colour. Usually it grows to about thirteen centimetres in length, but twenty-three-centimetre specimens are occasionally found. Two-thirds of its body and shell usually lie buried in the mud of the river bed, the foot projecting downwards to form an anchorage. Only the hind end with its inhalant and exhalant siphons can be seen protruding from the mud. Closely related to the swan mussel, and difficult to distinguish from it except that on the average it is smaller, is the duck mussel (*Anodonta anatina*).

Reproduction in the swan mussel and the other

freshwater mussels differs from that of the marine mussels. During the summer the female mussel produces thousands of eggs which instead of passing straight out into the water with the exhalant current are retained in special brood pouches among the gills. The males, however, do not retain the sperm, but allow it to pass out into the water, whence it is eventually drawn in by the female respiratory current and so makes contact with and fertilises the eggs.

The fertilised eggs remain in the brood pouch right through the winter, developing slowly, and eventually hatching out in the spring into special larvae known as glochidia. Each glochidium has a pair of tiny shell valves, and a single sticky byssus thread protruding between them. It is in this state that they are at last allowed to leave the protection of the parent shell. For a time they float about in the water, eventually settling to the bottom. On their way down, many of them get caught by their byssus threads and become entangled in water plants.

Further development is impossible as free animals. The only hope of survival for a glochidium is to become attached to a fish, for the next stage in its life history is parasitic. A fish swimming among the plants may brush against the glochidium, which attaches itself to the fish by its byssus and is carried away. Having been fortunate enough to find a host, the glochidium now proceeds to bury itself beneath the skin, or on the gills or fins, with the aid of a series of sharp teeth around the edge of the shell. The tissues of the fish react by forming a cyst around the glochidium, and in this cyst it can continue its development safe from its enemies and nourished by its host's blood.

Of course only a minority of the glochidia are fortunate enough to find a host. The vast majority wait in vain for a few days and then perish, having no means of obtaining food for themselves. The fortunate few remain within their cysts for about three months, during which time a new shell develops beneath the old one, and eventually they drop from the host to the pond or river bed as fully fledged young mussels.

Many freshwater fish serve as hosts to these freshwater glochidia, but the three-spined stickleback seems particularly prone to their attack. Sometimes there may be several dozen swellings on its fins and tail, each indicating the presence of a developing glochidium.

One fish, the bitterling, a native of rivers in continental Europe, has been established outside its natural range in a number of ponds, small lakes and canals in Britain and is a very popular garden-pond and aquarium fish. The bitterling gets its own back on the freshwater mussel. Instead of laying its eggs on the river bed, where they would be exposed to all kinds of predators, it deposits them inside the shell of the painter's mussel (*Unio pictorum*), where they can develop unmolested.

As the breeding season approaches, the egg duct of the female bitterling elongates so that she can insert it into the mussel shell and deposit her eggs in the mantle cavity, where they remain in safety until they hatch. Just as the baby fish are ready to leave the shell, the eggs of the mussel hatch out and the tiny glochidia are able to attach themselves to their minute hosts under the most favourable circumstances, being spared the period of waiting on a water plant on the off-chance of a fish passing close enough to become attached.

The pearl mussel (*Margaritifera margaritifera*) used to be a common sight in fast-flowing rivers, especially in Scotland, but populations have drastically declined and the species is now threatened with extinction. Habitat degradation is largely to blame, because the mussels depend on river beds covered in clean gravel. Human activities such as dredging introduce fine sediments which smother the gravel and cut off the supply of oxygen to young mussels. Pesticides and fertilisers washing off farmland can also impact pearl mussel populations. It is now illegal to gather pearl mussels, but poaching still takes place. The shell of the pearl mussel is relatively longer and narrower than that of the swan mussel, and rather smaller. Large specimens attain a length of between ten and thirteen centimetres. The presence of hinge teeth and its blackish colour distinguish it from the swan mussel.

That certain kinds of oysters produce pearls is common knowledge, but that pearls can also be found in mussels is less well known. Mussel pearls are formed in the same way as oyster pearls, a process which will be explained in the next chapter. Even in Roman times the British river pearl fisheries were famous, and right through to the eighteenth century considerable profits were made by pearl fishers on certain Scottish rivers, especially the Tay. From this river alone, £10,000 worth of pearls were sent to London during the years 1761–64. Mussel pearls vary in colour from white through pink, which are the most valuable, through green to brown and black.

Pearl fishing is now illegal but until a few decades ago was carried out in Scottish rivers, mainly by tinkers. They would wade slowly along the river bed, holding in one hand a glass box through which they could see the floor of the river, and carrying in the other hand a cleft stick with which to gather all large-sized mussels they found. These were collected in a sack, to be prised open with a knife at the end of the day. There was little money to be made out of mussel pearl fishing, however. The fisherman was lucky to find one pearl to every hundred mussels he opened, and only a small proportion of the pearls he did find had any commercial value.

Besides the swan and pearl mussels, we have several smaller species, which, like the swan mussel, are found only in ponds, lakes, canals and slow-moving rivers.

The painter's mussel (*Unio pictorum*) has already been mentioned. Its shell is long and thin, and up to seven centimetres in length. Its name is derived from the fact that Dutch painters at one time used the shells of this mussel as receptacles for their pigments. Gold and silver leaf used for illuminating manuscripts was also sold packed in these shells. Similar in size to the painter's mussel but with a thicker shell is the closely related swollen river mussel (*Unio tumidus*).

The last of our freshwater mussels is the zebra mussel (*Dreissena polymorpha*), which is quite different in its habits from all the other species, and in fact is more akin to the common mussel of the seashore. Like the latter, it produces a strong byssus with which it anchors itself to stones and other objects buried in the mud in the bed of the sluggish river, canal or lake in which it is found. Its name refers to the zigzag markings covering its yellowish-brown shell, which attains a maximum length of five centimetres. In its breeding habits, too, it is similar to the common mussel. Tiny free-swimming larvae are produced, which change to tiny mussels after a week or two of planktonic existence and sink to the bottom. These larvae are never parasitic.

The zebra mussel, unlike our other freshwater mussels, is not native to Britain. It was first discovered in Britain in 1824, in the Thames and in the waters of the Surrey Docks. Where it had come from no one was able to establish for certain, but it seemed likely that it had travelled across the North Sea from the Baltic attached to ships. From this initial introduction it has gradually spread through the freshwater systems of England and southern Scotland. Only in fast-moving rivers has it completely failed to establish itself, and this is probably accounted for by its method of reproduction. Planktonic larvae would be swept out to sea before they had time to change into young mussels and settle.

As zebra mussels continue to spread and increase in abundance, they cause significant economic and eco-logical damage. They build up in dense mats that can block water pipes in power stations and water-treatment plants. Each year, millions of pounds are spent on remov-ing hundreds of tonnes of zebra mussels from industrial installations, lakes and reservoirs. Native mussel species suffer and eventually die when zebra mussels settle on them, because they can't move, feed or breathe.

6

Oysters and Scallops

The aristocrat of all the molluscs, and economically by far the most important of them, is the oyster, one of the world's luxury foods and the provider of the vast majority of our pearls. Strictly speaking, it is a shallow-water species, but whenever it is found in offshore waters empty shell valves will be washed up on the shore.

In both structure and habit it shows several important differences from the common mussel. The anterior adductor muscle has been lost, the shell valves being closed by the contraction of the remaining posterior adductor muscle, which has moved forward to occupy a position near the centre of the shell. Generally it is found in sheltered bays and estuaries where the bottom is covered with rocks or stones, to which the left shell valve is firmly attached by means of a special cement.

When the free-living planktonic oyster larva or 'spat' changes to a young oyster and settles on to the sea or estuary bed it is provided with a foot on which it is able to creep about in search of a suitable rock or stone where it can spend the remainder of its life. A modified byssus gland then produces the adhesive cement, after which both the foot and the gland degenerate.

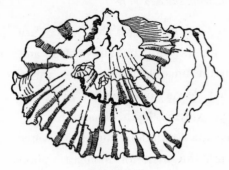

Lower valve

Lower valve

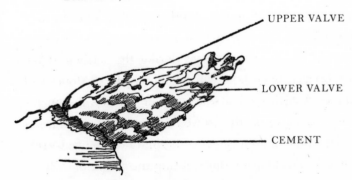

SADDLE OYSTER
Anomia ephippium
showing attachment
through lower valve

NATIVE OYSTER – *Ostrea edulis*
Both valves, from above

UPPER VALVE

LOWER VALVE

CEMENT

NATIVE OYSTER fixed to rock

FIG. 16: NATIVE OYSTER AND SADDLE OYSTER SHOWN
AT NATURAL SIZE

The oyster thus lies so that the two shell valves are one above the other, with the right one uppermost, and not side by side as in the mussel. These valves are of different shapes, the left (lower) one being convex and larger than the flat upper valve. Like the mussel, the oyster is a suspension feeder, a continuous current of water being drawn in through the posterior inhalant siphon and passed out through an exhalant siphon just above it after the diatoms and other minute organisms have been filtered out by passing the water through the gill meshes.

At the breeding season each female oyster produces as many as one million eggs, which are retained within the mantle cavity until they hatch to tiny ciliated larvae. The males shed their spermatozoa into the sea, and they are drawn into the female shell to fertilise the eggs with the inhalant current. When the larvae hatch they are allowed to pass out with the exhalant current, to spend several weeks floating about in the plankton. The majority of them are devoured by other creatures during this time, only a minority surviving to change into tiny oysters. There are further losses during the settling of the spat, because only those which fall on rocks or stones will survive. Any that fall on mud, sand or weeds will soon die, being unable to fix themselves. An interesting feature of the British species of oyster is its ability to change its sex, which it may do many times during the course of its life.

Most animals that live in the sea and on the shore are

very sensitive to temperature, which governs the limits of their distribution. Each species is adapted to life within a certain range of temperature, outside which it cannot survive indefinitely. Within this survival range is a narrower temperature range outside which it cannot breed. A particular species may thus be absent from a particular region not because the temperature is too high or too low for it, but because it is too warm or too cold for it to breed. Breeding activity, too, is linked with temperature. Spawning at the breeding season usually begins as soon as a certain minimum temperature is reached, and will continue so long as it doesn't fall below this lower limit again, or rise above the upper breeding limit. In the only species of oyster native to Britain (*Ostrea edulis*) spawning begins as soon as the water temperature in the spring rises to 15°C.

Until the middle of the nineteenth century our native oyster beds were able to supply all demands without resort to any special methods of oyster culture beyond throwing back empty oyster shells or 'cultch' to provide suitable additional surface on which spat could settle and develop. As requirements for the home market continued to rise, however, demand began to overtake supply, and the oyster fishermen began to look for methods of increasing the output of the oyster beds.

Many attempts were made to introduce the Virginian oyster (*Ostrea virginica*) from America and the Portuguese oyster (*Magallana angulata*) from the west coasts of Portugal. Young oysters about a year old were brought from their native beds and laid on British beds, where they flourished and grew to full size by the time they were four to five years old, thus growing at the same rate as *Ostrea edulis*. Neither species, however, was able to establish itself, because the colder waters of Britain never achieved the minimum temperature needed to stimulate their breeding activity. In consequence they produced no spat.

Greater success attended efforts to encourage Britain's native oysters. The idea of culturing oysters by providing artificial surfaces on which the spat could settle and grow is very old. Pliny records that the Romans achieved some success with artificial cultivation, but modern oyster culture owes most to France, where one would expect such a delicacy to be held in particular esteem. The stimulus to experiment was increased demand leading to serious depletion of natural stocks, which occurred during the middle decades of the nineteenth century. The extent of this depletion is shown by the fact that the beds in the Bay of Cancale, which in 1843 yielded seventy million oysters, were only providing about one million a year in the later 1860s, and the position had similarly deteriorated on all the other French oyster beds.

By this time, however, culture experiments were well underway. Bundles of brushwood were first tried as artificial spat collectors, but although the spat certainly settled on the wood, it was neither strong enough nor durable enough to survive the four or five years needed for the full growth of the oysters. Greater success attended the use of planks covered with pitch. When the young oysters were well attached to the pitch, it was broken away from the wood, which could then be recoated and used again. This method, however, was also found to have its drawbacks. A much more successful method discovered in 1865 involved the use of rounded roofing tiles coated with a mixture of lime and sand, which, as with the pitch, could be chipped off as soon as the spat was well established.

Using this method, the world's greatest oyster-rearing centre was built up in the Bay of Arcachon on the west coast of France. From this bay about ten thousand tonnes of oysters are produced every year, the majority being two-year-old oysters which will be re-laid on other beds to fatten for a further two or three years.

Oyster fattening has become in many places a separate industry from oyster rearing, with its concentration on spat collection. The most famous fattening beds are at Marennes near the mouth of the River Seudre. Here the oysters acquire a green colour due to the prevalence of a particular diatom. Although there is apparently no detectable difference between these green oysters and uncoloured ones, they are considered a particular delicacy in many places and command a correspondingly high price.

Originally all French oysters belonged to the species *Ostrea edulis*, but in modern times this has become almost completely replaced by the Portuguese oyster (*Magallana angulata*) on all the more southern beds. Its initial introduction to the French beds was unpremeditated. A cargo of oysters brought from Portugal went bad, and were thrown overboard near the mouth of the River Gironde. Some of these must have been alive and lived long enough to spawn, for a few years later a flourishing colony was discovered at the spot where the cargo had been jettisoned. Clearly the sea water over these southern beds attains a sufficiently high summer temperature to stimulate breeding activity in the Portuguese oyster. Further north, in Brittany, there are some of the last remaining populations of native oysters, *Ostrea edulis*. Like other oyster species, native oysters undergo a sex change, starting life as males and later becoming female.

The mid-nineteenth century was the heyday of the British oyster industry, when every year half a billion native oysters were harvested from the coasts and sent to Billingsgate Market in London. But by the beginning of the twentieth century, overfishing brought an end to the bonanza and the native oyster fishery collapsed. This trend is reflected in oyster species worldwide, where over the last century around 85 per cent of all oyster reefs and beds have disappeared – in Britain, 95 per cent of native oyster beds have gone.

With the lost oysters we have lost many important services they naturally used to provide for free, including filtering and cleaning water supplies. People around the world are now working hard to re-establish wild oyster populations, including native oysters in Britain, with projects underway in the Solent, Essex and South Wales. Restoration efforts include adding shell cultch to the sea bed and releasing adult oysters that are bred in captivity, which will hopefully spawn a new generation of native oysters in the wild.

A continuing problem are the various enemies of the oysters. As we saw in Chapter 3, these include two gastropod species: the American oyster drill (*Urosalpinx cinerea*) and the slipper limpet (*Crepidula fornicata*), which are predators and competitors respectively. As with the mussel, another of the oyster's enemies is the starfish. In earlier times, before the extraordinary regenerating powers of starfish were appreciated, the infuriated oyster fishermen used to tear to pieces every starfish that came up in their dredges, and throw the remnants overboard. They did not realise that they were contributing to the multiplication of their enemies, for every fragment would in a short time grow into a complete starfish.

A different kind of oyster pest is the boring sponge (*Cliona celata*), which establishes itself on an oyster shell and produces an acid secretion that gradually eats away the shell so that it crumbles to the touch. Oysters that have been attacked by the sponge are commercially valueless.

Excessive seaweed growth on oyster beds has the same effect as slipper limpets, smothering the oysters and restricting their supplies of water. By reducing the flow of water, deposition of silt is also increased. British oyster beds are all beyond the low-tide mark, but many French beds are exposed at low tide, and this enables the French oyster fishermen to use an ingenious method to keep down seaweed growth. Whenever this shows signs of becoming excessive, enormous numbers of common periwinkles are released on the beds to feed on the weeds. As soon as they have reduced the weed growth sufficiently, they are removed. If they were left after this time they would turn their attentions to the young oysters as soon as weeds became scarce, damaging their shells and reducing their future market value.

Although none of the three species of oyster dealt with here produces pearls, something must be said about the pearl oyster in view of the economic importance of the pearls it produces. Pearl oysters belong to the genus *Pinctada*. The majority of them are found in eastern waters, from East Africa to Australia and Japan.

What are pearls, and how are they formed? The innermost of the three layers forming the mollusc shell consists of a very smooth translucent material, which in members of the genus Pinctada and the genus *Margaritifera* is iridescent. It is in fact called nacre or mother-of-pearl and is separated from the outer layers to make buttons or other small objects. Occasionally a separate piece of mother-of-pearl, usually spherical in shape, is found lying between the mantle and the shell. This is the pearl of commerce, whose value depends upon its size, shape, colour and clarity.

An ancient Hindu belief attributed the origin of pearls to dewdrops which fell into the shells while they were open and were converted by the sun's rays. Their actual origin is much less romantic. They are formed by an accumulation of mother-of-pearl around any tiny foreign object that becomes lodged within the mantle tissue or between the mantle and the shell. Some of the latter are connected at one point to the shell. These are blister pearls of little value, though they are sometimes sawn off and used in cheap jewellery. Often the nucleus of a pearl is the egg or larva of a parasite, and sometimes an oyster's own egg may go astray and become the starting point for the formation of a pearl. Tiny grains of sand or other material can also initiate pearl production. Covering these particles with mother-of-pearl represents an attempt on the part of the oyster to reduce the irritation they cause by giving them a smooth and rounded coating.

In the past, pearl fisheries flourished in oceans around the world, including in Sri Lanka, the Red Sea, the Persian Gulf, Venezuela, Panama, the Philippines, Japan and the Gulf of Mexico. The fisheries were usually carried out by divers swimming down and gathering oysters by hand.

Today, wild-oyster fisheries have largely been replaced by cultured-pearl farms, an inevitability once people had invented a way of stimulating oysters to produce pearls on demand. The main hurdles were coming up with a technique that enabled oysters to be opened without damaging them, and finding particles which the oysters did not reject. The culturing process was developed by Englishman William Saville-Kent and first carried out at a commercial scale in Japan in the early twentieth century. The successful technique involves inserting between the oyster mantle and shell tiny pieces of mother-of-pearl wrapped in a tiny bag made from the fresh mantle tissue.

Pearls produced by oysters in response to this artificial stimulus are known as cultured pearls to distinguish them from the natural pearls that result from a naturally occurring stimulus. They are, however, true pearls, differing only from the so-called natural pearls in that the nucleus is a piece of mother-of-pearl and not a grain of sand or a minute egg or larva.

Cultured pearls are not cheap to produce or to buy. Huge numbers of oysters have to be collected from the beds by divers, and returned when the little packets of mother-of-pearl have been inserted. They must then be left for several years for the pearls to grow. Finally they are gathered again and opened. Nearly half of them will be found to have developed no pearl at all, and of the pearls found in the remainder only about one in ten will be of commercial value. China is currently the world's biggest producer of cultured pearls. In 2010 it produced twenty tonnes of saltwater pearls from oysters and 1500 tonnes of freshwater pearls from mussels reared in lakes, ponds and rivers. A single mussel can produce up to fifty cultured pearls at a time, one reason why freshwater pearls are much cheaper than those from saltwater.

The native oyster *Ostrea edulis* is the only true oyster in British waters, but there is also a small group of shore bivalves known as saddle oysters, which, despite their name, are not closely related to the true oysters. The common saddle oyster (*Anomia ephippium*) has a very flattened whitish shell irregular in shape but roughly spherical, and rather more than three centimetres across in a full-grown specimen. Inside, the shell is opalescent. The most obvious difference between saddle oysters and the true oyster is in their methods of fixing themselves to rocks and stones. The lower right valve of the saddle oyster is perforated, and through the hole passes a compact byssus which is hardened into a solid mass by being calcified. As the saddle oyster grows, the shape of its lower valve follows the contours of the rock to which it is attached, so that it offers the minimum of resistance to the movements of the water, a beneficial adaptation in a sedentary animal that has to resist the full force of the waves. Its powers of resisting desiccation, however, are limited, so that it is confined to the lower parts of the shore. Large numbers of young saddle oysters up to 1.25 centimetres in diameter are sometimes found adhering to spider crab shells. Because there is a superficial resemblance, fishermen once thought that saddle oysters were young stages of true oysters.

There are three other less well-known species of saddle oyster which are ribbed and yellowish white in colour, streaked or blotched with brown. They extend from extreme low-water mark into shallow water. Sometimes they are washed up attached to larger shells or to discarded crab shells. The most common of them is the ribbed saddle oyster, *Pododesmus patelliformis*.

More closely related to the oyster than these saddle oysters are the scallops, inhabitants of the shallow offshore waters, whose empty shells are frequently washed up on the shore. In their general mode of life they differ from most other bivalves. The bivalve typically is a sedentary animal, often using either cement or a byssus to fix it more or less firmly to rocks or stones. Some have adopted a burrowing habit, and are capable of limited movement through the sand or mud in which they live.

Most scallops, however, are active creatures, neither fixing themselves to rocks or stones nor burrowing in the sea bed, but capable of moving about freely and swiftly in the water.

When they come to rest on the sea bed they lie with the rounded and strongly ribbed right valve beneath, and the left valve, which is flattened in the edible scallop, on top. In this way the aperture is raised a little above the sand or mud and can draw in relatively clear water. As in the oyster, the anterior adductor muscle has been lost and the much enlarged and very powerful posterior muscle has come to occupy more or less central position. The two valves meet in a long hinge line formed by prominent lateral extensions of the shell called ears or wings. The hinge is provided with a strong elastic ligament which causes the valves to open widely when the adductor muscle is relaxed.

A head with eyes and other sense organs is very necessary for any animal that moves about, but is not so necessary nor so useful for a sedentary animal, which would be unable to move about in response to any stimuli received by these sense organs. We therefore find that many different groups of sedentary animals that have been evolved from active ancestors have in the process lost their special sense organs, and often their heads as well. The sedentary bivalve molluscs were derived from active ancestors, and in the process have lost nearly all trace of the head and its accompanying sense organs. Scallops, however, having again taken to an active life, have had to develop a new set of sense organs. They have not, however, acquired new heads. Instead, they have rows of short tentacles around the edges of the mantle folds, with numerous tiny eyes situated between their bases. Although these eyes represent a new development in the scallops, and not a continuance of the eyes possessed by the remote ancestors of the bivalves, they are well developed with lenses, retinas and nerves.

The scallop moves by closing its valves suddenly, the jet of water consequently forced out sending it through the water with a sudden jerk. This movement is not haphazard but can be controlled by varying the direction of the jet. The edges of the upper and lower mantles form a continuous curtain just inside the opening of the shell, and when the valves are closed by the sudden contraction of the adductor muscle the water is forced between the upper and lower halves of this curtain.

The curtain itself is muscular, and any part of it can be held rigid so that the water cannot be forced through it, and can only come out as a powerful jet where the curtain remains relaxed.

In normal swimming the scallop moves with the free edges of the shell foremost. This is achieved by relaxing the curtain on either side of the hinge so that the jet stream which is forced out at each rapid closing of the valves flows backwards at each side of the hinge line. The water is also directed slightly downwards because the upper curtain slightly overlaps the lower one, and this serves to carry the animal up from the sea bed. The intermittent nature of the jet means that the scallop proceeds by a series of jerks, sinking a little after each, the movement being very reminiscent of a butterfly in flight.

If suddenly disturbed by the approach of an enemy, the scallop is also capable of a different kind of escape movement. To achieve this it relaxes the curtains opposite the hinge line along the free margin, and is thus jerked into motion with the hinge foremost. With this movement the jet stream is not directed downwards, and so the animal does not rise upwards into the water, where it would be much more vulnerable.

By expelling water from only one side of the hinge line, the scallop can spin round. Sometimes it may be turned over in heavy seas so that the flat valve lies downwards. To right itself it directs a jet of water downwards from the free margin, and this serves to turn it over again.

Of the four scallop species inhabiting British waters, the largest is the edible scallop (*Pecten maximus*), whose shell may achieve a width of 12.5 centimetres. It is common and widespread in shallow offshore waters in many parts of the country. Next to the oyster it has the highest reputation of any molluscs with the gourmets.

The only other species that is eaten is the queen scallop (*Aequipecten opercularis*), about half the size of the edible scallop and distinguished from it by the fact that the upper as well as the lower valve is convex. It is most common along the south coast, where the majority of the landings are made.

EDIBLE SCALLOP – *Pecten maximus*

FIG. 17

Slightly smaller than the queen scallop, the variegated scallop (*Mimachlamys varia*) is distinguished by having unequal ears, while the fourth species, the humpback scallop (*Talochlamys pusio*), is not likely to be confused with any of the other three species. Its shell is irregular in shape, except when it is very young, and it does not swim about, but attaches itself by means of byssus threads to rocks or stones. Despite its sedentary habits, it does possess eyes like the other species, which suggests that it is descended from a free-swimming ancestor.

In its perfection of design and proportion the scallop shell is perhaps more beautiful than the shell of any other bivalve mollusc, and it is not surprising that it has been much used by artists from early times. In medieval times the scallop shell was adopted as the badge worn by pilgrims to show that they had visited Jerusalem.

Related to the scallops are the file shells, so called because the ribs on their white shells are so numerous and close together that the whole surface resembles a file. Like the scallops, they are capable of moving through the water, but are normally sedentary. The edges of the mantles are well supplied with tentacles, as are those of the scallop, but they are very much longer and project as a double fringe well beyond the shell valves, so that these have to remain permanently open. Movement through the water is brought about by a slow waving of these fringes of tentacles.

Since these tentacles cannot be withdrawn, and the valves have consequently to be kept open, the file shell is very much at the mercy of predators. To overcome this disadvantage it has learned to make a nest, a thing which no other bivalve is able to do. The whole shell is surrounded with a copious production of byssus threads to which sand grains, small stones, pieces of shell and seaweed, and other particles adhere. Openings are left through which inhalant and exhalant water currents can pass. Eyes are present on the mantle but are less well developed than those of the scallops.

In early life file shells swim about freely in the water like scallops, settling down to nest building and a sedentary life as they become adult. The largest and best-known British species is the gaping file shell, also known as the flame shell (*Limaria hians*), a very beautiful creature when seen alive, with its orange mantle and hundreds of orange filaments waving about in the water like the tentacles of a sea-anemone. In 2012, divers found a huge reef of gaping file shells in waters off the Isle of Skye in Scotland. Covering an area of sea bed of roughly seventy-five hectares (or about the same as three thousand tennis courts), it was made up of an estimated 100 million file shells.

7

The Common Cockle and Its Relatives

Although the mussel and the oyster are extremely successful animals, it is in the production of species that live
in sand and mud that the bivalve molluscs reach the peak
of their success. Many groups of seashore and marine
animals produce the odd unusual species that is adapted
for living buried in sand or mud, but the bivalves can
show a range of species and an abundance of individuals
unequalled by any other group. Unless they are deliberately dug out, these sand- and mud-burrowing bivalves
are seldom seen alive. Generally we see only the empty
shells washed up in great numbers on the beach. These
represent the shells of those that have died, and in most
cases the movement of the water has separated the two
valves, so that these are found singly. As we walk over
the lower parts of a sandy or muddy shore when the
tide is in, few of us realise what an immense population
of bivalve molluscs and other creatures may be living
beneath our feet.

Perhaps the best known and certainly one of the most
successful and abundant of these hidden bivalves is the
common cockle (*Cerastoderma edule*), which will provide
an excellent example to introduce the group. Most of

the structural differences between the cockle and mussel can be related to the differences between their modes of life. The mussel leads a sedentary life, fixed firmly to the rock by its strong byssus threads, but the cockle, though it spends its time buried a couple of centimetres or so below the surface of the sand, is mobile and fixed to nothing. It therefore produces no byssus, but its foot is a well-developed, powerful organ with which it can plough its way through the sand, horizontally or vertically, with considerable speed. If a cockle is washed up to the surface, or dug out from the sand when the tide is out, its foot can be used to carry it along in a series of little jumps. To achieve this leaping movement the foot is first bent in the middle while the tip is pressed down onto the sand. It is

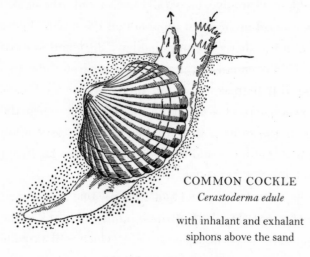

COMMON COCKLE
Cerastoderma edule

with inhalant and exhalant
siphons above the sand

FIG. 18: NATURAL SIZE

then straightened suddenly like a spring being released, and then the animal is sent either rolling along the sand or upwards into the water or the air.

Like the mussel and the oyster, the cockle is a suspension feeder, taking in a continuous current of sea water and filtering out from it the microscopic plankton organisms suspended in it. Because it lies buried, however, its inhalant and exhalant siphons extend beyond the edge of its shell in the form of two tubes which are joined together along most of their length.

The cockle lies in the sand in such a position that these siphons lie more or less vertically, with their external openings on or slightly above the surface of the sand. Both openings are fringed with a ring of filaments.

With its prominent radiating ribs, the cockle shell is one of the most easily recognisable of all bivalve shells. These ribs possibly help the cockle to grip the sand and prevent it sinking too far below the surface. The group name Cardium, which is common to all cockles, refers to the heart shape of the closed shell when looked at endwise, a resemblance it owes largely to its very prominent umbos or beaks.

On a really good cockle bed the population density is well-nigh incredible. As many as 3,750,000 cockles to the hectare are known to exist on some beds extending for several hundred hectares. The cockle's method of reproduction is precisely similar to that of the mussel.

Reproductive products are shed into the sea, where fertilisation of the eggs takes place. From these hatch minute larvae which spend the first few weeks of their life as members of the plankton. Many of them eventually settle on sand or firm mud, which will be their final home, but great numbers take up temporary residence in areas of soft oozy mud that is unsuitable for adults to live in. Here they remain for a time while further development takes place, later migrating to more suitable ground where they can spend the remainder of their lives.

In certain parts of the country fishing for cockles is quite a flourishing industry, including the Thames and the Wash. In 2004 there was a tragedy in Morecambe Bay in Lancashire when twenty-three Chinese cockle pickers were cut off by the incoming tide and drowned.

Cockles have been gathered from Bury Inlet, near Swansea in South Wales, from Roman times onwards. Since then, the techniques have barely changed. Around fifty licensed gatherers rake cockles from the mud at low tide. The cockles are then sieved and any small enough to fall through the mesh are left in place to rebury themselves in the mud. In 2001, Bury Inlet became the first bivalve fishery awarded an eco-label by the Marine Stewardship Council, meeting standards for sustainable fishing. Surveys are carried out twice a year to determine harvest levels and make sure enough cockles are left behind to breed and feed birds such as oyster catchers.

In addition to the prominent radial ribs, the cockle shell also shows a number of concentric growth lines. During the summer, while food is plentiful, shell is laid down rapidly, sometimes at the rate of a millimetre or more every week, but in winter there is very little growth. This winter growth shows as a narrow ring in contrast to the much wider ring laid down during the summer. The number of winter rings thus indicates the number of winters through which the cockle has lived. Unfortunately this method of estimating the age of a cockle is not completely reliable. If for some reason food is short for a few weeks during the summer months, rings similar to winter rings are formed. These disturbance rings, however, are often less prominent than the annual winter rings.

In his book *A Year at the Shore*, published in 1865, Gosse refers to the great abundance of the common cockle on the beaches around the islands of the Outer Hebrides, and of the importance of the cockle harvest to the inhabitants of these islands.

It is on the north-western coasts of Scotland, however, that the greatest abundance of these mollusca occurs, and there they form not a luxury, but even a necessity of life to the poor semi-barbarous population. The inhabitants of those rocky regions enjoy an unenviable notoriety for being habitually dependent on this mean diet. 'Where the river meets the sea at Tongue', says Macculloch, 'there is a considerable ebb, and the long sand-banks are productive of cockles in an abundance which is almost unexampled. In a year of scarcity they presented every day at low water a singular spectacle, being crowded with men, women and children, who were busily employed in digging for these shell-fish as long as the tide permitted. It was not unusual also to see thirty or forty horses from the surrounding country, which had been brought down for the purpose of carrying away loads of them to distances of many miles. Without this resource, I believe it is not too much to say, that many individuals must have died for want.'

Except for the oyster, molluscs are regarded by many people as a very inferior kind of food, fit only for the poor in wealth or taste. In fact they are a highly nutritious and well-balanced kind of food, containing an abundance of protein, fat and glycogen, or animal starch. One oyster is the equivalent in food value, both quantitatively and qualitatively, of one glass of milk.

Besides the common cockle there are some half a dozen other cockle species found around our coasts. The largest of these is the spiny cockle (*Acanthocardia aculeata*), whose shell frequently exceeds eight centimetres across, as compared with the maximum breadth of five centimetres for the common cockle. The red colour of its foot distinguishes it from the common species, and provides an alternative name 'red noses'. It is local in its distribution, occurring only in the south-west, where it extends from the low-tide mark well out to sea. Gosse has left an interesting account of the red noses or Paignton cockle. In his day, the sandy beaches of Torbay were celebrated for their abundance of these large cockles.

Indeed, the species is scarcely known elsewhere; so that it is often designated in books as the Paignton cockle. A right savoury *bonne bouche* it is, when artistically dressed. Old Dr Turton, a great authority in his day for Devonshire natural history, especially in matters relating to shells and shell-fish, says that the cottagers about Paignton well know the red noses, as they call the great cockles, and search for them at low spring tides, when they may be seen lying in the sand with the fringed siphons appearing just above the surface. They gather them in baskets and panniers, and after cleansing them a few hours in cold spring-water, fry the animals in a batter made of crumbs of bread. The creatures have not changed their habits nor their habitats; for they are still to be seen in the old spots just as they were a century ago: nor have they lost their reputation; they are indeed promoted to the gratification of more refined palates now, for the cottagers, knowing on which side their bread is buttered, collect the sapid cockles for the fashionables of Torquay, and content themselves with the humbler and smaller species, the common cockle.

The spiny cockle is easily distinguished from the common cockle. Its shell has more red on it, especially around the margin, and it has only twenty or twenty-one ribs as against between twenty-four and twenty-eight in the smaller species. Along each rib, too, there is a single row of prominent sharp spines. The bright red foot is considerably larger than the pink foot of the common cockle.

Similar to the spiny cockle is the prickly cockle (*Acanthocardia echinata*), a smaller species in which the spines on the ribs are less well developed, and the shell of a paler yellow colour with much less red. Its foot is pink like that of the common cockle. Prickly cockles are widely distributed on sandy shores all round our coasts.

Another large species whose shells are found only on our south-western shores from Dorset to Cornwall is the rough cockle (*Acanthocardia tuberculata*), which is similar in size to the spiny cockle but with a coarser and more solid appearance. The ribs have fewer spines, and these are blunt and flattened. The animal itself lives in the sea bed below the offshore waters, and so cannot be dug up on the beach like the preceding species.

Distinctive again is the smooth cockle (*Laevicardium crassum*), whose forty or so ribs are so little developed that the shell feels nearly smooth. It is a widely distributed shallow-water species whose whitish shell mottled with faint pinkish-brown tinting is commonly washed up on many beaches.

The five previous species are all of fair size, varying from four to eight centimetres in diameter when full grown. Our remaining three species are much smaller, with shells which seldom exceed 1.25 centimetres across. None is a shore species, so that only empty shells will be found washed up on shore from the shallow offshore waters beneath which they live. All three are widely distributed in British waters. The little cockle (*Parvicardium exiguum*) has a yellowish-white solid-looking dull shell with about twenty flattened ribs, and lives in soft sand or mud just beyond the low-tide mark. The banded cockle (*Parvicardium pinnulatum*) lives in gravelly sand in anything up to 150 metres of water. Its name is derived from the series of prominent reddish-brown concentric bands on the shell distinguishing it from the other small species. Very similar to it, but lacking the banding, is the knotted cockle (*Parvicardium scabrum*), which lives in sand or gravel. Knotted and banded cockles both have more delicate shells than the little cockle.

Related to these seashore cockles, though not very closely, is a group of tiny freshwater bivalves consisting of orb-shell cockles (*Sphaerium* species) and pea clams or pill clams (*Pisidium* species). They have thin, almost globular, pale-coloured shells, which can be easily mistaken for small pebbles as they lie on the bed of pond or river. Both groups are widely distributed and well represented in all kinds of fresh water. The orb-shells average about 1.25 centimetres in diameter, and the best known of the four species is the horny orb-shell (*Sphaerium corneum*). Although small, orb-shells are very active, and able to move about using a well-developed foot. Often they are found climbing about on weeds in the water, and they can also use it to float at the surface of the water, the body and shell being suspended beneath it. At the onset of winter they bury themselves in soft mud, remaining in hibernation until the water warms up again the following spring.

Fertilisation of the eggs takes place while they are still within the shell. They are then retained within a brood pouch until they hatch, and the young continue to remain there for some time, only passing out through the exhalant siphon into the surrounding water when they have developed enough to take care of themselves.

Pea clams are even smaller than orb-shells, some species not exceeding six millimetres in diameter. They are distinguished from the orb-shells by possessing only a single siphon instead of the pair of siphons characteristic of bivalves in general, otherwise they are similar in appearance and habits. Fifteen species are known from British waters.

Both orb-shells and pea clams are sought after by fish and by ducks and other water birds. They have evolved a most ingenious method of migrating from one place to another on the feet of water birds. While the bird's feet are in the water, the molluscs close their valves tightly in such a way as to grip a piece of the skin on the sole of the bird's foot. When the bird takes to the air, the clinging bivalve is taken with it, releasing its grip only when the bird alights on another stretch of water. By this method, isolated ponds and lakes can be colonised and their populations reinforced, thus ensuring maximum distribution.

8

Rounded Shells in Variety

Among the most common of the bivalve shells that you will find on any beach are the various kinds of venus shells, carpet shells, tellins, wedge shells, trough shells and a few smaller groups, comprising in all several dozen species. All these shells are roughly circular in outline, similar in fact to cockle shells but lacking their characteristic ribs. Although at first sight they may all look too much alike for the different kinds to be easily distinguished from each other, closer examination shows that each group has its own characteristic features. Like the cockles, they are typically inhabitants of the sand or mud of the seashore or the shallow seas, the depths to which they burrow depending upon the length of their siphons. A majority of them live buried in the sea bed beyond the extreme low-tide mark, so that the complete animals cannot be dug up. Separate valves washed in by the tides are all you can hope to find.

External examination of a selection of these rounded shells shows that they can be divided into two groups: those which are completely smooth, and those whose surface is raised into a series of ridges concentric with the umbo. The latter group comprises the ocean quahog, the heart cockle and the venus shells.

The ocean quahog (*Arctica islandica*) is one of the largest of our bivalves, the thick shell of a full-grown specimen measuring up to thirteen centimetres across and almost as much from beak to margin. Instead of rising straight up from the hinge line, the beaks are distinctly curved towards the front edge of the shell. The actual colour of the shell is white slightly tinged with pink or yellow, but this is masked by a thick brown epidermis. Numerous prominent concentric ridges arranged close together cover the whole shell. So convex are the two valves that when the complete shell is viewed end on it appears heart-shaped, the two prominent beaks forming the top of the heart. Ocean quahog shows a preference for muddy sand beneath shallow

OCEAN QUAHOG – *Arctica islandica*

FIG. 19: NATURAL SIZE

water, lying only just buried so that its short siphons can project above the surface. A well-developed foot suggests that it moves about a good deal. It is widely distributed, so you might find it washed up on almost any beach, but nowhere is it very common. Ocean quahogs are some of the longest-lived animals on the planet. In 2013, scientists calculated that they can live for more than five hundred years.

Even more closely resembling a heart when looked at from one end, because its valves are more convex, is the heart cockle (*Corculum cardissa*). The curvature of the beaks, too, is more exaggerated, and the surface of the valves carries a smaller number of better-developed ridges. It is a slightly smaller shell than the ocean quahog, large specimens measuring up to ten centimetres

HEART COCKLE – *Corculum cardissa*

FIG. 20: NATURAL SIZE

across. The shell itself is thick and yellowish white, but, like the ocean quahog, is covered externally with an epidermis, which is reddish brown in colour. Heart cockles are confined in the main to the south-west and west coasts, where they live just buried in mud in shallow water beyond the low-tide mark, and even here they are not very common.

The venus shells are all smaller than the heart cockle and the ocean quahog, and the beak is not turned towards the anterior end to the same extent. A well-developed foot and less convex shell valves enable them to sink into and move through sand quite rapidly. Their shell colour is not obscured by an epidermis as it is in the two larger species. Venus shells vary in abundance and in the extent of their distribution around our coasts.

The one whose shell you are perhaps most likely to find, being both widely distributed and abundant, is the striped venus (*Chamelea striatula*). Fully grown, it measures a little more than 2.5 centimetres across. Its colour is pale yellow, with three reddish-brown rays each consisting of a rather irregular line of blotches and passing across it from beak to margin. The surface of each valve is sculptured with a considerable number of quite prominent, roughly concentric, ridges. Whereas most of the venus shells live in offshore waters at depths varying between a few metres and about two hundred metres, the striped venus can be found beneath the sand in the region of the extreme low-tide mark, where the complete animal can therefore be dug up. Its slender siphons are rather longer than those of most other venus species.

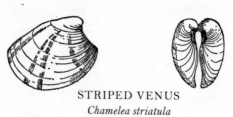

STRIPED VENUS
Chamelea striatula
FIG. 21: NATURAL SIZE

Slightly smaller and darker in colour, varying from yellow to reddish brown and carrying a variable number of darker rays, is the banded venus (*Clausinella fasciata*). It too is widely distributed and abundant, and also occurs on the lowest parts of the shore, where it lies both in sand and in gravel. The ridges are fewer but better developed than those of the striped venus, and the siphons are shorter.

Smallest of all the venus shells is the oval venus (*Timoclea ovata*), which seldom exceeds 1.25 centimetres in diameter. It is really a shallow-water species, but may occasionally be dug out from the sand at extreme low water. Unlike the other venus shells, the surface of its valves is raised into some forty to fifty-five ribs radiating from beak to margin, and crossed by the usual concentric ridges, which are more prominent and about twenty in number. The colour of the oval venus is yellowish tinged and blotched with pink and brown.

Besides these three small and widely distributed species there are several larger species of more restricted distribution. The pale venus (*Venus casina*), whose colour varies from whitish to pale brown, is about five centimetres in diameter, with very prominent ridges. Nowhere is it abundant, but it is found in a number of widely separated areas, living on sandy sea beds where the water is between ten and two hundred metres deep. Slightly larger is the warty venus (*Venus verrucosa*), whose drab brown shell has a very rough appearance due to the fact that each of its prominent ridges is raised into many wart-like irregular knobs. It is confined to the south and west coasts where it lives offshore in both sand and gravel.

Largest of all the true venus species is the smooth venus (*Callista chione*), whose thick shell, up to ten centimetres across, may be found washed up on the shores of Cornwall. As its name suggests, the ridges are so little developed that the shell is practically smooth. Pinkish brown in colour and very glossy, as though covered with a coat of varnish, and with a number of darker rays extending from beak to margin, it is one of the most attractive of all our bivalve shells. The animal itself lives in sand beneath fairly deep water off the coast of Cornwall. Sometimes after a heavy storm the whole animal may be torn from the sea bed and washed up on the beach.

Besides the six venus species already described, which are native to British waters, we also have an alien species,

Mercenaria mercenaria. This is an American species which was first recognised here around the mouth of the Humber in 1864, since when it has proceeded to spread along the east coast. How it was first introduced no one knows. In America it has considerable commercial value as an edible species, being known as the soft clam, to distinguish it from the hard clam, which will be described in Chapter 9. Unlike the latter, it does not occur in such dense colonies, and no attempts have been made to cultivate it. The name *mercenaria* refers to the fact that it was one of the shells used by the North American Indians for making 'wampum' or strips of beads that they used for money.

Closely related to the true venus shells are three other species. The so-called wavy venus (*Mysia undata*) is ridged like typical venus shells, but is much thinner and almost transparent. It is widely distributed and lives beneath sand in shallow offshore waters. The shell, which seldom exceeds 2.5 centimetres in diameter, is white in colour, tinged with yellow near the beak.

The two kinds of artemis shells, the rayed artemis (*Dosinia exoleta*) and the smooth artemis (*Dosinia lupinus*) both have shells whose margins are more nearly circular than those of true venus species. Both are yellowish white in colour. The rayed artemis shell approaches five centimetres in diameter, and has numerous well-developed ridges and several faint reddish-brown rays and irregular spots. It lives buried in offshore waters in sheltered sandy bays. Ridges are less numerous and less well developed on the somewhat smaller smooth artemis, which is found on sandy ground from the extreme low-water mark, and so can sometimes be dug up at low spring tides.

Although also quite closely related to the venus shells, the four species of carpet shells can be distinguished from them both by their shape and their colour. The beak is rather less prominent than in most venus shells, and is less obviously turned towards the front, though it is situated well forward, near the front edge, a feature which distinguishes the carpet shells from all other bivalves of similar general shape. From the beak the hinge line continues almost as a straight line, and not as a curve, so that the whole shape of the shell is less circular and more like a square or rectangle with rounded corners. They owe their name to the irregular distribution of various coloured markings all over the surface of their shells, suggesting the pattern on a carpet. Carpet shells have somewhat longer siphons than venus shells and cockles, and this enables them to be buried a little deeper in the sea bed.

The speckled carpet shell (*Venerupis corrugata*) and the cross-grained carpet shell (*Venerupis decussata*) are both common species living in muddy gravel low down the shore, where they can be dug up in considerable numbers, and extending into shallow water. Both are about four centimetres in length and carry a file-like pattern

formed by the intersection of numerous shallow furrows
running both horizontally and vertically. The speckled
carpet shell has a yellowish-white ground colour splashed
with irregular purple and brown patches. In the cross-
grained carpet shell the colouring is similar but the
patches are less prominent, and the shell is more mark-
edly square than oval. The cross-hatching, too, is better
developed, so the surface has a rougher texture. On the
continent, considerable quantities of these two species
are eaten.

SPECKLED CARPET SHELL   THICK TROUGH SHELL
Venerupis corrugata   *Spisula solida*

FIGS. 22 AND 23: BOTH SHOWN AT
NATURAL SIZE

In contrast, the banded carpet shell (*Polititapes rhom-
boides*) has a glossy smooth shell. The splashes of purple
and brown which overlay the yellow ground colour are
arranged in several somewhat irregular vertical bands
instead of being scattered haphazardly about the shell
surface. Banded carpet shells live in sand beneath shallow water, only occasionally being dug up low down the
shore.

The fourth species, *Venerupis saxatilis*, has unusual habits. Unlike the majority of the bivalves considered in this and the previous chapter, it does not burrow into the sea bed. Instead it lives in rock crevices and in the holes made by the various rock-boring bivalves described in Chapter 9. Correlated with this unusual mode of life, they have retained the power of producing byssus threads with which to fix themselves. In appearance they are similar to speckled carpet shells, but with a more irregular outline.

Trough shells can be distinguished from venus shells and carpet shells by the fact that the beak is centrally placed and not turned to one side, and the hinge line curves away from either side of it, giving the whole shell approximately the shape of a triangle with the corners rounded. The surface of the shell is smooth and glossy with a series of fine concentric lines etched on it. Even when the valves are closed, they gape slightly at the hind end, so that the siphons can never be completely covered when they are withdrawn. The foot is well developed, enabling the trough shells to burrow into and move quickly through the sand in which they live. Like the cockles, they can also use it for leaping.

There are two groups of trough shells: *Spisula* species, with thick solid shells; and *Mactra* species, which have thinner and more delicate shells. One of the most common species is the thick trough shell (*Spisula solida*), which is found all round our shores living in gravel and sand from extreme low-tide mark into shallow water. The full-grown shell is four to five centimetres across, and yellowish white in colour. Very similar to it, but little more than half the size, is the elliptical trough shell, which is relatively rather broader as its name suggests. It lives in deeper water further away from the shore.

The cut trough shell (*Spisula subtruncata*) is relatively deeper and less broad than the other species, its general shape suggesting the head of a hatchet. It is a sand dweller, and extends from the low-tide mark well out to sea in moderately deep water. A smaller species than the previous two, its greyish-white shell measures up to 2.5 centimetres across. In certain places it occurs in incredible numbers over enormous areas, and plays a major part in feeding particular flatfish, whose diet consists almost entirely of the various invertebrates that live on and buried beneath the sea bed. In the 1950s, extensive *Spisula* beds were known from Dogger Bank in the North Sea. The beds of bivalves extended for many square kilometres, with a density of several thousand molluscs living beneath every square metre of the sea bed. Since then, these beds seem to have declined, possibly because of shifts in the climate.

The rayed trough shell (*Mactra stultorum*) is of similar shape and size to the thick trough shell, but it has a thin glossy yellowish-white shell traversed by a number of reddish-brown rays running from the beak to the margin.

It burrows in sand from the low-water mark out to depths of about forty metres, and is widely distributed around our coasts but not particularly common anywhere.

A larger species of more limited distribution is the glaucous trough shell (*Mactra glauca*). Its thin shell has similar colouring to the rayed trough shell, but the rays are lighter. During life it is covered with a shiny brown epidermis. Full-grown shells may measure up to 7.5 centimetres across. In Britain it is found only in the south-west, mainly on sandy Cornish beaches, where it can sometimes be dug up near the low-water mark during spring tides.

All the bivalves so far considered in this and earlier chapters are suspension feeders, filtering out the suspended plankton organisms from the inhalant current of water. There are, however, four important groups of sand- and mud-burrowing bivalves that have perfected a different method of feeding. On the surface of the sand and mud there is always a layer of organic material that settles down from the water, and it is these organic deposits that the deposit feeders gather up for food. To enable them to obtain this material while lying buried beneath the surface they have long thin flexible inhalant siphons, which can extend for fifteen centimetres or more beyond the hind end of the shell. These siphons are moved over the surface of the sand with the opening facing downwards, the deposited organic material being sucked in with the inhalant water current rather like a vacuum cleaner picking up dirt along with a current of air. The exhalant siphon is quite separate from the inhalant siphon in order to allow the latter maximum freedom of movement, and is usually shorter because it does not have to extend beyond the surface of the sea bed.

The wedge shells can be distinguished from other groups dealt with in this chapter mainly by their shape. They are relatively broader and less deep than any of the others, their shape being roughly that of a long narrow rectangle with, of course, the corners rounded. They are fairly thick robust shells, which distinguishes them from the thin delicate shells of those tellins that might otherwise be confused with them. They are among the most highly polished and attractive of all our bivalves.

Best known of them, and one of the most beautiful, is the banded or purple-toothed wedge shell (*Donax vittatus*), a brightly coloured but variable shell about 2.5 centimetres across. Yellow, brown and purple specimens are known. Several concentric bands of deeper tint than the ground colour pass across the shell, which often has three rays of white passing vertically down it. Numerous finely scored lines radiate from the beak, but fade away before reaching the margin. The banded wedge shell lives only just beneath the surface from low-water mark to shallow water in sandy bays, where it often occurs in considerable numbers.

PURPLE-TOOTHED WEDGE SHELL
Donax vittatus

FIG. 24: NATURAL SIZE

For a deposit feeder it has quite a short inhalant siphon, about 2.5 centimetres long. The alternative name, purple-toothed wedge shell, refers to the fact that the edges of the valves are serrated or milled with many small tooth-like projections. Wedge shells are quite active animals, with the foot well developed for swift movement. The valves, in contrast to the convexity shown by many of the suspension feeders, are much flattened, so that end on the animal looks very thin. Their slenderness and smoothness both facilitate swift movement through the sand.

The only other species of wedge shell likely to be picked up on British beaches is the polished wedge shell (*Donax variegatus*), whose distribution in our waters is virtually confined to the coasts of Devon and Cornwall, where it may extend from low water to a depth of several metres. Its high-polished shell is chestnut-brown crossed with a few cream-coloured rays. The most obvious difference between the two species, though, is the fact that the valves of the polished wedge shell have smooth margins in contrast to the serrated edges of the banded wedge shell.

Similar in shape to the wedge shells, though much thinner and more delicate, are the tellins, of which there are several British species, all sand burrowers. The valves are so flattened that there seems scarcely room between them for a complete mollusc body. They, too, are equipped with a well-developed foot and are able to plough quickly through the sand. Deposit feeders need to change their positions more frequently than suspension feeders. The continuous movement of the sea means that fresh supplies of food are always being brought to the suspension feeders, which might well spend the whole of their lives in one position and never lack sufficient food. Once a deposit feeder has sucked up all the deposited organic material within reach of its inhalant siphon, however, no further supplies can be obtained until further settling has occurred, and this may take some time. Movement to another spot therefore becomes necessary in order to obtain fresh supplies of food. Hence the flattened highly polished shells, without ribs or ridges which would impede movement through sand or mud, and the well-developed powerful foot, which are characteristic of all deposit-feeding bivalves. The ribs and ridges found on the shells of many suspension feeders, and the frequent convexity of the valves, giving a rather broad appearance to the whole animal when viewed end on, also represent adaptation. They help to fix the animal in its chosen position in the sea bed, and prevent it either sinking too deep or being washed out by the continual movements of the water.

The most common and most widespread of all the deposit feeders is the thin tellin (*Macomangulus tenuis*), a tiny shell seldom exceeding 1.25 centimetres in length. Its valves, whose colour varies from white or yellowish white to pink or yellow, are so thin as to be almost transparent. Tellins burrow deeper than wedge shells and so have longer siphons. Most of the bivalves featuring in this chapter are really shallow-water species whose empty shells only are ever washed up on the beach. The range of a few of them extends up to or a little higher than low-tide mark, where they can be dug out at low

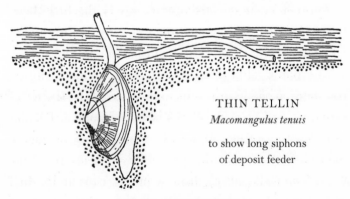

THIN TELLIN
Macomangulus tenuis

to show long siphons
of deposit feeder

FIG. 25: NATURAL SIZE

water during spring tides. The thin tellin, though, is a true shore species, extending as far up the shore as the neap tide high-water mark and downwards into shallow water up to about five metres deep, but reaching its peak of abundance on the lower parts of the shore. Here it sometimes occurs in dense beds containing a thousand or more individuals beneath every square metre of sand.

The blunt tellin (*Arcopagia crassa*) is distinguished from other species by the possession of a number of concentric ridges like those found on most venus species. It is larger than most tellins, attaining a maximum length of five centimetres. The colour of the shell is white tinged with yellow and with a number of red streaks. It is really an offshore species which can, however, sometimes be dug out from the sand at extreme low water. The inhalant siphon is nearly four times as long as the exhalant.

Another common offshore species is the little bean tellin (*Fabulina fabula*), of similar size to the thin tellin. Its pearly white shell carries faint pink or yellow.

The Baltic tellin (*Macoma balthica*) is found living on the shore in sandy gravel or mud, often in the shelter of estuaries, and in many places is very common. Population densities of more than five thousand to the square metre have been recorded in muddy estuaries. It is very variable in its colouring, from white to crimson. Its shell is thicker and less flattened than those of the majority of deposit feeders. This is probably correlated with the fact that on the surface of the mud in which it lives there is more available food than there is on a sandy surface, and therefore it does not have to move about as much as sand burrowers do.

The third group of deposit feeders are known as sunset shells and like the wedge shells and tellins they are also sand burrowers. They, too, have long, narrow and extremely flattened shells, but unlike those of the other two groups they gape slightly at the hind end, like the trough shells, and they also have a more angular appearance. The name sunset refers to the arrangement of the colouring on the shell. Rays of pink or red radiate from the beak like conventional representations of the sun's rays at sunrise or sunset.

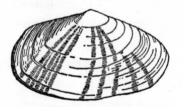

LARGE SUNSET-SHELL
Gari depressa

FIG. 26: NATURAL SIZE

The largest of them, and the one most likely to be found on the shore, is sometimes known as the large sunset-shell (*Gari depressa*). It is about five centimetres long, with pink or purple-brown rays crossing the pale yellow ground colour.

Compared with the shells of most other deposit feeders it is rather thick and less glossy. In common with other sunset shells, its colouring is somewhat masked by a greenish epidermis, which may become worn away. Slightly smaller is the Faroe sunset shell (*Gari fervensis*), which has a pinkish ground colour and crimson rays. At the hind end the valves are squared off rather sharply.

Whereas the three groups of deposit feeders so far considered are, in the main, sand burrowers with the odd species found in mud or muddy sand, the members of the fourth group, the furrow shells, are adapted for life in mud. Most of them are found in greatest abundance in estuaries where the water is brackish. Their most striking feature is the great length of the inhalant siphons, which are very much longer than those of any other deposit feeder, and very thin. All the furrow shells are white or greyish-white in colour, more or less oval in shape, and thin. At the hind end, in common with the trough and sunset shells, there is a slight gape even when the valves are fully closed.

The most common and best-known species is *Scrobicularia plana*, one of the largest of all deposit feeders, whose oval shell may grow to five centimetres in length. In some parts of the country it is known as the mud hen. Although its shell is very flattened and its foot well developed, it seldom changes its position, for, as already mentioned, there is more food available on mud than on sand. It is never found on open shores, but only in estuaries where the water is brackish. Here it is a true shore species living between the tide marks. In this kind of habitat concentrations of one hundred to the square metre are common. As the tide goes out the siphons are withdrawn and the animal sinks fifteen to twenty centimetres below the surface. With the return of the water it comes up again to lie only just buried so that its fifteen-centimetre inhalant siphon can sweep a considerable area of mud.

There are several other species of furrow shells all similar to *Scrobicularia plana* in shape and colouring but

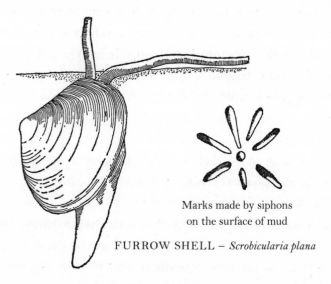

Marks made by siphons
on the surface of mud

FURROW SHELL – *Scrobicularia plana*

FIG. 27: NATURAL SIZE

very much smaller, seldom attaining even 1.25 centimetres in length. Most important of these are the thin furrow shell (*Abra tenuis*) found in the mud of many southern estuaries, mostly beyond the low-tide mark; the prismatic furrow shell (*Abra prismatica*), an uncommon offshore species inhabiting sandy mud; and the white furrow shell (*Abra alba*), a mud dweller from low-water mark in estuaries and sheltered creeks.

To complete this survey of the rounded bivalve shells we must look briefly at five small groups of suspension-feeding bivalves, most of them having but one or two British representatives. The first group contains a single species, the northern lucina (*Lucinoma borealis*), an almost round white shell up to four centimetres across, scored with a series of concentric ridges and covered with a yellowish-brown epidermis. It lives in gravel and muddy sand beyond the low-water mark, and extends outward to a depth of about two hundred metres. A long narrow foot serves to anchor the animal as it lies either on or just beneath the surface.

Another somewhat smaller shell, with a squarish outline, *Diplodonta rotundata*, is also the sole British representative of its group. This, too, is a white shell with concentric ridges and is covered with a yellowish epidermis. It lives mostly off our southern and western shores in or on sandy mud beneath several metres of water a little way offshore.

The third group consists of two species, *Kellia suborbicularis* and *Lasaea rubra*, which are particularly interesting because of their viviparity. The fertilised eggs are retained within the mantle cavity while they pass right through the larval stages, only leaving when they have finally changed to young bivalves able to lead a similar mode of life to the adults. Both are tiny white shells, of globular shape, and almost transparent, *Kellia* being about eight millimetres long and *Lasaea* about three millimetres. A thin iridescent epidermis gives the shells a greenish sheen. The larger species lives just beyond the low-tide mark, in discarded shells, under stones and among the holdfasts of the tangleweeds, as well as buried in mud. *Lasaea* is, however, a true shore species, where it lives in rock crevices, among seaweed fronds, and indeed anywhere it can find sufficient shelter.

Lepton squamosum, the coin shell, is the single representative of the fourth group. It is a small white oval shell, about 1.25 centimetres long, semi-transparent and glossy. Coin shells are quite rare, and have an unusual and restricted choice of home. In sand and gravel from the lowest-tide mark on sheltered bays three kinds of so-called burrowing prawns make their homes, which consist of deep permanent burrows each having several openings to the surface. *Lepton* also lives within the shelter of these burrows and is found nowhere else.

The most interesting in their habits of all these five

groups are the Montagu shells, named after the Colonel Montagu who discovered them. These tiny bivalves, all under six millimetres in length, spend their lives attached to various species of sea urchins or sea-cucumbers, in an association of the kind known as commensalism, in which two different species live together and share the same food. *Montacuta substriata* and *Tellimya ferruginosa* are two species that live on heart urchins, to whose spines they are attached by byssus threads. These heart urchins are sand burrowers, and obtain their food supplies by swallowing enormous quantities of sand and digesting the organic material present in it. The Montagu shells attach themselves near the mouth of the urchin so that they can extract food particles from the sand as it streams towards its mouth. Both are white or yellowish white, with a well-developed foot.

Devonia perrieri attaches itself to sea-cucumbers by means of a sucker developed on the surface of a much enlarged foot which is equal in size to all the rest of the body. This is a very tiny species scarcely more than two millimetres long.

9

Bivalves that Bore into Wood and Rock

Many marine animals, including quite a number of molluscs, burrow into the sand or mud on the sea bed in order to hide from their enemies, and a few have so perfected the burrowing technique that they are able to excavate permanent tunnels for themselves in wood or rock. The majority of these rock- and wood-borers are bivalve molluscs. Economically some of these are of great importance because they are able to do considerable damage to wooden ships, pier and jetty piles, and the stonework of harbours and breakwaters.

The chief offender among these boring molluscs is the shipworm, well known from Greek and Roman times as a destroyer of ships. Aptly named by Linnaeus 'Calamitas navium', but now called *Teredo navalis*, the shipworm is a good example of an animal that has become so modified in structure in adapting itself to an unusual mode of life that its true family relationships are only revealed through its life history. Yet despite its worm-like appearance and its name, it is nevertheless a bivalve mollusc.

Adult shipworms are found only in infected wood, their extreme specialisation making it impossible for

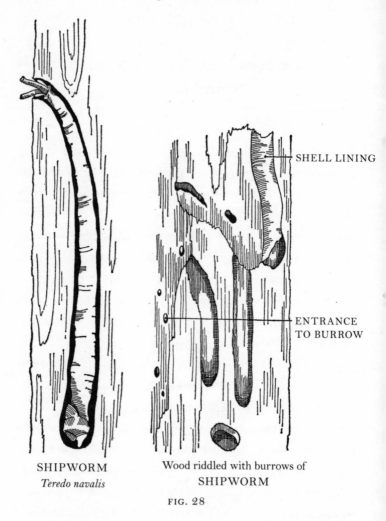

SHELL LINING

ENTRANCE
TO BURROW

SHIPWORM
Teredo navalis

Wood riddled with burrows of
SHIPWORM

FIG. 28

them to survive anywhere else. Each worm occupies a
burrow which opens at the surface as a mere pinhole, but
below it widens out to the diameter of the worm, which

will be about six millimetres in a full-grown specimen. At the inner end of the burrow is the front end of the worm, carrying two small and much modified shell valves which the worm uses in excavating its burrow. The outer surface of each valve is raised into numerous rows of tiny sharply pointed teeth, making it a most efficient rasp or file.

These valves are of course much too small to enclose the shipworm or even the front end of it, and the adductor muscles, instead of being used to close the valves, are modified in such a way that their contraction rocks the two valves from side to side. The foot, too, is modified to a sucker-like organ which grips the sides of the burrow while the valves are held tightly against its inner end. As they are rocked, they scrape away the wood and so extend the burrow. It is said that the scraping of the shells as they rasp away at the ends of their burrows can be heard by placing the ear against wood in which they are working. As a seventeenth-century writer quaintly put it, 'They gnaw with their teeth and pierce into Okes, as you may know by the noise.'

The hind end of the long body is fixed to the burrow just inside the tiny opening, through which two narrow tubes can be protruded or withdrawn at will. These are the inhalant and exhalant siphons. A respiratory current of water drawn in through the one passes out through the other after having passed through the gills. The long tube connecting the front and hind ends of the body is really an elongated gill chamber, the gills forming a septum between the inhalant and exhalant currents. The plankton extracted from the water by the gills and passed forward to the mouth constitutes only a part of the shipworm's diet. It is able to digest and obtain nourishment from the particles of wood scraped off during boring operations. It does this with the aid of bacteria living symbiotically inside its gills.

When disturbed or alarmed, the shipworm can withdraw its siphons and close up the entrance to its burrow with two small plates of shelly material. Similar material is produced by the shipworm to line its burrow. Sometimes the surface of badly infected timber is worn away, leaving these shelly linings still intact and projecting as much as several centimetres above the new surface.

However many shipworms there may be in a piece of timber, each one carefully avoids running its burrow into another one. A close examination of infected timber will usually show examples in which a worm has stopped excavating and sealed up the end of its burrow with shelly material just before it would have penetrated another burrow. In such cases the worm has often withdrawn a few centimetres and then started boring again in a different direction.

It is in its life history that the shipworm shows its molluscan features most clearly. Like so many marine molluscs, it sheds its reproductive products into the exhalant current, whence they are passed into the sea. A temperature trigger mechanism ensures that all shipworms in the same neighbourhood will spawn more or less together, so that there will be a high concentration of eggs and spermatozoa in the surrounding water, thus ensuring a high proportion of fertilisation. The tiny ciliated larvae which hatch from the eggs within a few days are very similar to those of other bivalve molluscs. For a time they remain in the plankton, and then each changes into a minute but unmistakable bivalve with a pair of shell valves, a prominent foot and a single byssus thread produced by the byssus gland.

At this stage, although still about 0.25 millimetres long, it begins to settle and to search for a piece of wood. Of course the vast majority of the larvae will settle where there is no wood, and these will perish within a day or two. Those that do fall in the vicinity of wood, however, seem to be aided in their search for it by some chemical sense, for experiments have shown that these minute shipworms are definitely attracted by both wood and an alcoholic extract of wood.

Once it is settled on a piece of wood, the tiny creature attaches itself by means of its single byssus thread and begins to bore as fast as it can, rocking its shell valves to and fro while holding them firmly against the surface of the wood. In a very short time it has worked its way right into the wood and disappeared from sight, leaving only a tiny hole at the surface to betray its presence.

Growth and change now take place rapidly. The shell valves become modified as rasps and the hind end of the body fixes itself just inside the burrow. As the tunnelling proceeds and the burrow lengthens, the worm-like middle section of the body appears and grows in length to maintain the connection between the advancing front end of the body, containing most of the internal organs of the shipworm, and the siphons, which remain at the entrance to the burrow.

The young shipworm is able to grow very quickly. A specimen under observation at Plymouth attained a length of twenty-eight centimetres in about eight months. Their rapid rate of growth, coupled with their methods of attacking wood, make shipworms very formidable pests to deal with. The pinhole openings which the larvae make are very difficult to detect, so that an apparently solid pile may in fact become reduced inside to a mass of shipworm burrows separated only by thin layers of wood, while the surface looks quite sound. Each larva, too, needs such a tiny area for sinking its initial burrow that a very large number can enter through a small exposed surface of wood.

Numerous methods of protecting submerged wood from shipworm attack have been tried, but none has proved completely successful. The Greeks and Romans often sheathed the hulls of their triremes and galleys with lead plates, and other metals have been employed in more recent times. Paints and various other compositions have also been used to cover wood and so protect it from the larvae, while pier piles are often encased in a layer of concrete or cement. The trouble with all these methods is that sooner or later a little of the wood surface becomes exposed through damage to the covering and so the larvae can get at the wood.

In piers and harbours scupper-nailing has also been extensively used. Large numbers of broad-headed iron nails are driven in all over the submerged surface of the wood. Rust from these spreads out over the whole surface, and acts as a deterrent to the settling larvae, being distasteful if not actually harmful to them. Impregnation with creosote has also been tried with some success, but applications have to be repeated periodically because it is slowly washed out by the sea water.

Although the larvae cannot develop into adult shipworms unless they settle on wood, they are able to survive for several months, so that during the summer there are large numbers of them drifting about in the sea. Consequently, any unprotected timber stands a very good chance of becoming infected. Another unfortunate feature of these shipworms is their ability to remain alive for a fortnight or more when a ship is dry docked, and so continue their devastating work when the ship gets back to sea again.

The damage caused by the shipworm through the ages must have been very great. Greek triremes, Roman galleys and the great wooden ships of medieval and later times all succumbed to its ruthless attacks. Many a famous old ship that survived a lifetime of storms and battles was finally destroyed by the insidious but ruthless attacks of the mollusc. Drake's *Golden Hind* foundered at her final anchorage in the Thames near Woolwich when her timbers became riddled with countless shipworms. There is a piece of ancient oak timber in the British Museum riddled with shipworm borings. It was taken from the remains of the wreck of an old sixteenth-century ship in this area, which may well have been the *Golden Hind*.

The attacks of the shipworm on the dykes of Holland in the eighteenth and nineteenth centuries more than once brought the country to the verge of disaster. These attacks were periodic. For some considerable time little or no damage would be caused because of the virtual absence of shipworms. Then would come a disastrous year when myriads of shipworm larvae would appear and attack almost every piece of submerged timber.

These periodic outbreaks in the Zuiderzee are believed to have been connected with periods of low rainfall. *Teredo* is not able to live in water whose salinity is less than five parts per thousand, and can only lead a fully active life when the figure exceeds ten parts per thousand. (The average salinity of sea water is thirty-five parts per thousand.) Many harbours built on estuaries are therefore comparatively safe from shipworm attacks because the fresh river water keeps the salinity low. The years of excessive *Teredo* outbreaks in the Zuiderzee have always followed periods of abnormally low rainfall, which presumably allowed the salinity to rise above the minimum required for full *Teredo* activity, by reducing the amount of fresh water brought in by the rivers.

The most serious outbreak of modern times occurred in San Francisco Bay between 1914 and 1920. Before it was finally checked, damage estimated at ten million dollars had been caused.

There is perhaps just one thing that can be said in favour of the shipworm. It was by studying its methods of boring that Sir Marc Isambard Brunel conceived the idea and the method of constructing a tunnel under the Thames. Helped by his more famous son, Isambard Kingdom Brunel, it took him eighteen years to complete, from 1825 until 1843.

Besides the common shipworm there are two other species of *Teredo* found in British waters. *Nototeredo norvagica*, the Norway shipworm, is larger than the common shipworm, and its shell is pale brown and not white as in the smaller species. It is not so widespread as *Teredo navalis*, and confines its attentions in the main to fixed timbers, leaving floating timber and ships alone.

Psiloteredo megotara is sometimes known as the drifting shipworm, because although it may occasionally be found in fixed timbers, it is generally found only in driftwood cast up on the shore. It is also called the big-ear shipworm on account of its shell being ear-shaped. In size it is intermediate between the other two species. Some tropical species of shipworm are very much bigger than those found in cooler waters, the largest specimens attaining a length of about 1.5 metres and the thickness of a man's arm.

Floating timber washed up on the shore is sometimes found to contain burrows made by another kind of wood-boring bivalve called *Xylophaga dorsalis*. This has two shell valves similar to those of the shipworms, and it bores its way into the wood in the same way. Also like shipworms, *Xylophaga* extracts nourishment from the wood, and it may gain some nutrients from bacteria living inside it. It bores only for protection. The burrows, too, are shallow, so that the animal remains just beneath the surface of the wood, and there is no long worm-like tube connecting the siphons with the remainder of the body within the shell valves. Shipworms can only exist in wood because they rely on it for their food, but specimens of *Xylophaga* sometimes excavate their homes in the insulating layers of submarine cables.

A number of different kinds of bivalves have perfected methods of excavating tunnels in rock, where they live and enjoy considerable protection from their enemies. Best known perhaps are the piddocks, of which there are several British species. They are certainly the most highly developed and efficient of our rock-borers.

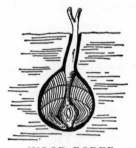

WOOD-BORER
Xylophaga dorsalis
FIG. 29: NATURAL SIZE

The piddock is a gaper, its valves remaining apart at both the front and hind ends. Through the front gap the foot, modified as a sucker, can be protruded to grip the inner end of the tunnel, while through the gap at the opposite end the siphon tubes are extended. No ligament binds the two shell valves together. At the front ends the valves carry rows of minute teeth with which the rock is worn away as the burrow is excavated or enlarged. To do this the piddock takes a firm grip with its foot and then rocks and twists the whole shell by alternate contraction of the anterior and posterior adductor muscles, both of which are well developed. Absence of a hinge ligament allows independent movement of the two valves. All the time the valves are pressed firmly against the rock. When it first bores its way into the rock the piddock is quite a small specimen, so the opening to the burrow is not usually very big. Inside, however, it is bigger, because as the piddock grows it is able to widen as well as lengthen its burrow. Sometimes piddocks burrow quite deeply into the rock, and to compensate for this their siphons are capable of considerable extension to enable them still to reach the mouth of the burrow to draw in the respiratory water current.

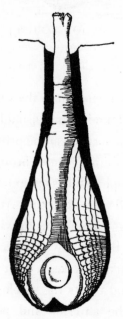

COMMON PIDDOCK – *Pholas dactylus*

FIG. 30: NATURAL SIZE

The piddocks' boring mechanism must be very efficient, because they are found in almost any but the very hardest rock, though they do tend to be more common in the softer sandstones, shales and chalk. Despite the hard work that they have to do, the shell valves are quite thin, but they are very strong. One very curious fact about piddocks is that although they spend virtually the whole of their lives hidden away in rocks, they are among the most strongly phosphorescent marine animals, the whole surface of the body being suffused with a powerful greenish-blue light.

In contrast to the care taken by the shipworm to avoid breaking into another's burrow, the piddock seems to carry on in the direction it has chosen without any consideration for its fellows in the same piece of rock. Gosse has recorded an instance of one piddock not only meeting but boring right through the body of another.

A lady, watching the operation of some Pholades [piddocks] which were at work in a basin of sea water, perceived that two of them were boring at such an angle that their tunnels would meet. Curious to ascertain what they would do in this case, she continued her observations, and found that the larger and stronger Pholas bored straight through the weaker one, as if it had been merely a piece of chalk.

The largest of the several piddock species that are found in rocks around our coasts is the common piddock

(*Pholas dactylus*), which may be as much as fifteen centimetres long when full grown. Each valve carries up to fifty rows of sharp teeth, which are most prominent towards the front end of the valve. In the region where the two valves meet, and where in a normal bivalve the hinge ligament would be found, there are two additional plates of shell lying side by side, known as dorsal shields. These provide additional attachment for the very powerful muscles of the foot. Behind them are two more smaller plates lying one behind the other and giving some protection to the mantle and the margins of the valves in this dorsal region. Besides boring into all kinds of rock, the common piddock will also excavate its burrows in wood and peat.

The white piddock (*Barnea candida*) is about half the size of the common piddock, but is found in similar materials. It can, however, be distinguished by the fact that it has but a single dorsal plate in place of the four possessed by its larger relative. Slightly smaller again is the little piddock (*Barnea parva*). It also has only a single dorsal plate, but its shell is more compressed than that *of Barnea candida*. It is, too, mainly confined to our southern and south-western shores.

Zirfaea crispata, the oval piddock, has a shell which is more oval and less rectangular in outline than that of the previous three species. Its single dorsal plate is reduced to a tiny triangle of shelly material.

The last member of the group is the paper piddock (*Pholadidea loscombiana*), which differs considerably from the other species both in structure and habits. Its shell is very thin and delicate, and at the hind end extends as a horny cup to surround the base of the siphons. There are two dorsal plates, but in older specimens these may have fused together. Unlike other piddocks, it stops boring after a time, and its foot degenerates. The paper piddock is more limited in its distribution than any of the other piddocks, being confined to south-western England and parts of southern Ireland, where it is usually found in sandstone on the lowest parts of the shore.

In Chapter 3 mention was made of certain alien mollusc species accidentally introduced to British waters when attempts were made to establish the American oyster on our beds. Among these introductions was an American species of rock-boring bivalve (*Petricolaria pholadiformis*). The first introduction is believed to have occurred about 1890 on the east and south-east coast beds. Although similar in its habits to the piddocks, it is not closely related to them.

Smaller than the piddocks, but no less common around our shores, are two species *Hiatella rugosa* and *Hiatella arctica*, the former growing to about four centimetres long while the latter seldom exceeding this length. The shell valves, which gape at each end like the piddocks, are roughly rectangular in shape, and devoid of fine teeth for scraping rock. Instead, they are coarsely wrinkled. The name 'red noses' by which these two species are commonly known refers to the colour of their siphons, which are seen at the entrance to the burrow.

ROCK-BORER
Hiatella arctica

FIG. 31: NATURAL SIZE

They are much less specialised for burrowing than the piddocks, and in fact will often be found not in rocks but living on the surface among mussels or the holdfasts of tangleweeds, where they anchor themselves by byssus threads. How they form their burrows, which are generally in limestone but more rarely in sandstone, is not known with any certainty.

It has been suggested that the repeated closure and contraction of the siphon tubes forces water into the body and so presses the valves slightly apart against the rock, which is by this means gradually worn away. Despite the apparent crudity of this method, they are nevertheless able to excavate burrows as neat and as deep as those produced by the better-equipped piddocks. The larger species more often lives in burrows than the smaller one.

Although in earlier times it was sometimes suggested that these various rock-boring molluscs were aided chemically in their operations by producing liquids which would soften or eat away the rock, all the species so far considered do in fact rely entirely upon mechanical means to excavate their burrows. There is, however, one kind of bivalve that does make use of chemical action in burrowing. It is the date mussel (*Lithophagus lithophaga*), a Mediterranean species that is not found as far north as our shores. In colour, size and shape it is similar to a date.

A special gland produces acid which is able to dissolve limestone and chalk. Its method of boring limits its distribution, because since the acid would have no effect on non-calcareous rocks, the date mussel is never found in these. Special provision has to be made to protect its own calcareous shell from being attacked by the acid, and this is achieved by providing it with a complete additional outer layer of horny material. The shell itself, not having to stand up to mechanical boring, does not need to be so tough as the shells of other rock-borers, and is in fact quite thin and delicate. It is an interesting fact that in closely related bivalves which do not burrow, the special acid-producing gland is absent.

In parts of the Mediterranean region, ancient borings made by date mussels thousands of years ago provide unusual evidence of the rise and fall of land. The best-known example is at Pozzuoli near Naples. Here, the limestone pillars of the Roman market building, or macellum, are still standing, and for several metres up they are riddled with date-mussel burrows. Certainly, when the macellum was built it was on dry land, as it is today. But during the intervening years the land must at some time have sunk sufficiently for it to be covered by the sea to a depth of several metres, when the date mussels carried out their excavations. Later still, the land rose again to bring the macellum out of the water once more.

Besides the rock-borers there are several other groups of gapers which burrow into the sea bed for protection, and whose general mode of life is similar to that of the cockle. Siphon tubes project a little above the sea bed to take in a current of clean sea water. Most of them have elongated shells of similar proportions to those of the piddocks, with the elongation carried to extremes in the razor shells.

One of the largest of all our bivalve molluscs is the common gaper (*Mya arenaria*). Full-grown specimens measure some fifteen centimetres long and 7.5 centimetres broad. The siphons, which are connected throughout their length, can if necessary be contracted completely within the shell, but are capable of being extended as much as a foot beyond the hind end of the shell. Their ends are fringed with a prominent circle of tentacles. *Mya* burrows deeply, usually lying about twenty centimetres below the surface of the sea bed, and long siphons are necessary to reach the water above it. The tips of the siphons lie flush with the surface of the sand, usually in a slight depression, which makes them easier to detect.

The shell valves bear prominent, roughly concentric ridges, and are covered with a dark-greyish horny outer layer, which continues as a sheath over the siphons. *Mya* is widely distributed, and often occurs in great numbers, preferring muddy sand or gravel, especially in estuaries, where it is quite tolerant of brackish water. When the animal is dug up, it visually contracts its siphons completely. In some parts of the country it is used for food under the alternative name clam. It is, too, the common soft clam of America, where large numbers are eaten, and densely populated natural beds are systematically fished. Young clams are imported from other regions, and re-laid on these beds to increase the populations. Originally found only on the Atlantic coasts of America, the clam has been introduced into San Francisco Bay, where extensive and flourishing beds have developed.

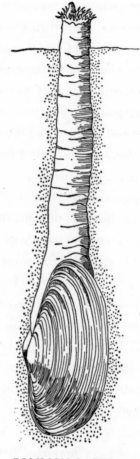

COMMON GAPER
Mya arenaria

FIG. 32: ×0.5 NATURAL SIZE

Young gapers move about freely and have a relatively large foot which can produce byssus threads for
temporary attachment. As they grow, however, they eventually bury themselves, sinking gradually further into the
muddy sand as they get bigger, their siphons elongating
correspondingly. Once established in the sand, the gapers
will not normally move about or come to surface again for
the rest of their lives. Their feet, having thus done their
work, do not continue to grow with the rest of the body,
so that in full-grown specimens they are relatively small
and useless. If a gaper is dug up and left on the sand, it can
slowly work its way down again, but it takes several hours
to regain its original depth. Lying as deeply as it does, it is
unlikely in the normal course of events to be thrown out
of its burrow, even by the stormiest seas, so that inability
to burrow quickly is really no handicap to it.

The blunt gaper (*Mya truncata*) is a somewhat smaller
and less common species. In general structure and mode
of life it is similar to the common gaper, but the hind end
of the shell is flattened or truncated, and looks as though
it might have been sawn off. It is found in stiff mud as
well as in muddy sand.

Very similar to the gapers in appearance and habits
are two species of otter shells. The common otter shell
(*Lutraria lutraria*) is nearly as big as the common gaper,
and lies at similar depths in sand or mud from extreme
low-water mark into shallow water, which makes it rather

difficult to obtain. Its yellowish-white shell is much lighter than the gaper shells. The oblong otter shell (*Lutraria oblonga*) is a smaller species with a relatively more slender shell. In general habits and distribution it is similar to the larger species, the main difference being that the inhalant siphon is very much longer than the exhalant, suggesting that it is a deposit rather than a suspension feeder.

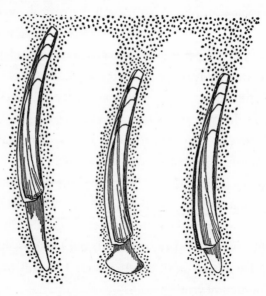

RAZOR SHELL – *Ensis ensis*
to show how it uses its foot to sink through sand
FIG. 33: NATURAL SIZE

Of all the bivalves that burrow in sand, none are better adapted to this kind of life than the razor shells, and no others have so perfected the art of moving fast through it. Razor shells are quite unmistakable. The largest species (*Ensis siliqua*) is about seventeen centimetres long and 2.5 centimetres or more wide. The sides of each valve are straight and parallel, and the ends almost straight and approximately at right angles to them, the whole shape approximating to a long narrow rectangle. Both valves are alike and meet all along their sides, but gape widely at the hind end to allow passage for the siphons, and at the front end for the well-developed, powerful foot. *Ensis ensis* is a somewhat smaller species whose shell is slightly curved. Both have similar habits and distribution.

Razor shells are widely distributed on sandy shores near the low-water mark, lying vertically with their siphons directed upwards and feet downwards. When covered by the tide, they move up towards the surface so that the ends of their short siphons project slightly into the water. As the tide recedes, they go deeper, remaining quiescent some little way below the surface until the tide returns. Other sand- and mud-burrowing bivalves can be easily dug out with a spade, but not so the razor shells. The slightest vibration causes them to sink at an amazing speed and the only hope of obtaining a specimen is to approach with extreme caution to avoid vibrating the sand, and then to plunge a spade right into the sand and throw out the sand all in one movement. Even so, more razor shells will be missed or cut in half than are dug out whole. The position of a razor shell beneath the surface is often betrayed by a slight depression in the sand at the surface.

The slender shape of the shell and its extreme smoothness both help it to move swiftly, but the most important factor is the efficiency of its foot. This is very large, and when retracted it occupies at least half of the space enclosed between the two shell valves. When the razor shell wants to go deeper, it protrudes its foot vertically downwards. Since it is pointed, it slides easily through the sand. When it is fully extended, blood is pumped into the tip, which swells to a mushroom shape to form a firm anchor. The rest of the foot is then contracted, the whole shell thus being drawn down towards the swollen tip, which is then allowed to contract to normal proportions as the blood flows back into the body. To move upwards, the foot is extended only a short way before the tip becomes swollen. As extension continues, the shell is pushed upwards. Upward or downward movements can be repeated several times to cover greater distances than can be achieved by one extension or contraction of the foot.

Although in normal circumstances a razor shell will probably not leave the sand, violent storms may throw it onto the surface. If so, the foot proves an extremely efficient instrument for returning it to the sand. As the

animal lies along the surface of the sand, its foot is protruded and turned downwards, being pushed into the
sand as far as it will go. The tip is then distended as it
contracts again. This will carry the front end of the shell
into cover, and another similar movement will usually
carry the whole shell out of sight. A study of a related
species, the Atlantic jackknife clam (*Ensis leei*), revealed
that, while burrowing, they repeatedly open and close
their shells, causing the hard sediment surrounding them
to collapse. Water then seeps inwards, creating a pool of
liquidised mud or quicksand, which reduces the drag on
the shell and increases burrowing efficiency tenfold.

There are two other British species of razor shell
which you are less likely to find, *Solen capensis*, whose
shell is more tubular in shape than those of the *Ensis* species, and *Pharus legumen*, the pod razor, so called because
it is shaped like a long pod. Both lead a life similar to
that of their better-known relatives.

10

The Octopus and Its Relatives

Although we have now met all the molluscs that have a shell in the ordinary sense of the word, no account of shells on the shore would be complete without reference to the most highly developed of all the molluscs: the squids, cuttles and octopuses which comprise the class Cephalopoda. And although it has lost the ancestral shell altogether, we shall begin with a description of the octopus, which is not only the best-known representative of the group, but is one of the most remarkable creatures in the whole animal kingdom.

No one would guess by looking at an octopus that it belonged to the same group of animals as the oyster and the snail. Yet fundamentally its body is built on the same plan as that of the gastropods. The eight arms or tentacles surrounding the mouth are developed from the gastropod foot. They are broad where they leave the body and taper to fine flexible tips which the octopus can use with considerable precision to extract meat from the dismembered crabs and lobsters which are the principal items in its diet. A membrane connecting the bases of the arms helps the creature when it is swimming and also provides folds in which captured prey can be imprisoned until required.

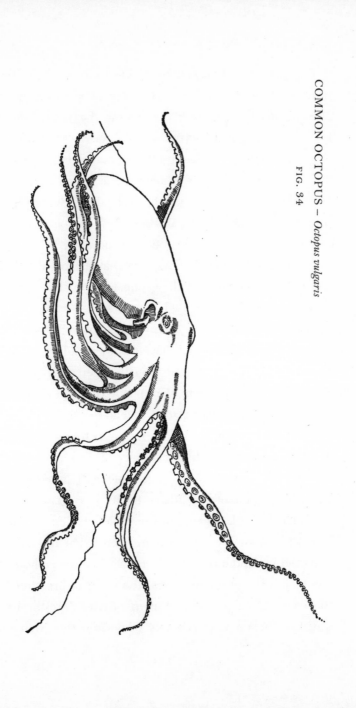

COMMON OCTOPUS – *Octopus vulgaris*

FIG. 34

The suckers, arranged in a double row along the under-surface of each arm, are also graded in size from 2.5 centimetres or more in diameter at the base to about 1.5 millimetres at the extreme tip. Each sucker consists of a ring of muscle with a fleshy disc in the centre. When the arm is used to grip an object, the suckers are first pressed flat onto it, and then the fleshy disc is withdrawn, creating a vacuum. With all its suckers, an octopus has considerable gripping power at its command.

Its body is an entirely fleshy bag, having lost the shell that is a characteristic of the group, and which its ancestors undoubtedly possessed. A good-sized specimen of the common octopus (*Octopus vulgaris*), which visits our south-western shores, will have a body about as big as a coconut and an arm span of about 1.5 metres. In a really large individual, the arm span may extend to about 2.5 metres, with a body the size of a small football.

The other important features of an octopus are a pair of rather staring eyes, better developed than in any other invertebrate animal and comparable with our own in efficiency; a pair of formidable horny jaws very similar to a parrot's beak, and capable of inflicting a painful bite, though seldom used defensively even when the animal is picked up; and a respiratory tube called the siphon. In common with other molluscs, the octopus breathes by means of gills kept within a mantle cavity. A respiratory stream of water is alternately taken into this cavity to sweep over the gills, and expelled through the siphon, just as we inflate and deflate our lungs. If you watch an octopus at rest, you can see the breathing movements.

Unlike its relatives the ten-armed squids and cuttles, which are aggressive hunters of the open seas, the octopus is essentially an in-shore animal, preferring a quiet life. During the daytime it prefers to remain hidden away in some rock crevice near the extreme low-tide mark on the shore or in the shallow water beyond, coming out at night to hunt for food.

When it does stir, it has a choice of three ways of moving. Sometimes it walks slowly along the sea bed in a rather ungainly manner on its arms. At other times it rises into the water and swims by gently waving its arms about, the thin web joining the arm bases being of considerable help in this movement. But if it is really in a hurry, it can move backwards very quickly by a type of jet propulsion. By quickening up its breathing movements it can send out a series of waterjets from its siphon, each capable of shooting it two or three metres through the water.

Crabs and lobsters are its favourite food, and it is for these that it goes hunting at night, rising into the water and descending like a cloud over any unfortunate crab it encounters. Even when hiding in its lair during the daytime, it remains on the alert for any unsuspecting crab which may happen to pass, flicking out one of its arms to touch the crab lightly as soon as it comes within reach. Then a curious thing happens. The crab raises itself on its legs and holds up its claws, a typical offensive attitude, as though it is going to attack the octopus arm. But that is as far as its defensive instincts take it, for it appears to be in some way hypnotised by the octopus, which without further trouble is able to capture it and tuck it away in the folds of its arm webs.

The crab may be kept alive for some time while others are collected. One octopus was observed to collect no fewer than seventeen crabs before settling down to its meal. To get at the crab meat, it pulls off the arms and legs, using the flexible ends of its arms to extract it and pass it into its mouth. An octopus lair is often discovered through the heap of empty crab shells lying around the entrance.

The octopus has a well-developed brain, and is credited with many feats of intelligence. Joseph Sinel, a marine naturalist of an earlier generation, who was very familiar with the octopus and its ways, related seeing an octopus kill a small rockfish and place it outside its lair as bait to attract unwary crabs. He also records an interesting observation on the memory capacity of the octopus. Some hungry captive specimens were offered oysters. For many hours the oyster shells were patiently explored with the tips of the arms, but no method of entry could be found, and the attempt was finally abandoned. A week later, more oysters were offered to them, but after a momentary glance, no further interest was shown in them.

Lobsters are more difficult for the octopus to catch than crabs, because they are not frightened of it. It is of course the lobster's claws which are the danger. Once the octopus has managed to grip these, the lobster is vanquished, but a prolonged battle of wits may occur before a really big lobster is overpowered. A story is told of an aquarium octopus which escaped from its own tank and managed to find its way to the tank in which the lobsters were kept. The largest lobster, a really magnificent specimen, engaged the octopus in a battle lasting many hours. By nightfall neither combatant had achieved any advantage over the other. Next morning, though, the keepers arrived to find the octopus sleeping peacefully surrounded by the empty shells not only of its previous day's opponent, but of those of all the other occupants of the tank as well.

Because of its partiality for crabs and lobsters the octopus can be a menace to fishermen. Around the Channel Islands and off the north-west coasts of France it is usually fairly common during the summer. Its numbers vary, however, and sometimes reach plague proportions. In 1899 and 1900 the crab and lobster fisheries in these areas were completely ruined by an octopus plague, which extended to British shores and affected our fisheries in the latter year.

Increases in the octopus population always follow a series of warm summers, which provide favourable conditions for such a warm-water species to breed at the northern limits of its range. Increases in the octopus populations on both sides of the Channel in 1949 and 1950 were attributed to several warm summers in preceding years. In-shore fishermen in Devon and Cornwall all too frequently hauled in their lobster pots to find them occupied by an octopus surrounded by the empty shells of what should have been a good catch of lobsters. After the Second World War, the Guernsey States Committee for Agriculture set up artificial lobster hatcheries as a means of maintaining the lobster populations in the face of the depredations of the octopus.

Fisheries data show that from the second half of the twentieth century onwards, the abundance of octopuses and other cephalopods has increased worldwide. Various factors may account for this, including overfishing of other species, mainly fish, that are competitors or predators of octopuses. Cephalopods may also be faring well and reproducing faster with the increased sea temperatures associated with anthropogenic climate change.

In a 1954 report on his investigations into the distribution of the octopus in British waters, Dr W. J. Rees, of the British Museum, suggested that our population does not breed here, but is maintained by a yearly immigration of paralarvae carried by currents from the breeding areas further south. The larvae which hatch from octopus eggs are now known to live for some time in the plankton before settling down on the sea bed.

Although the octopus is able to terrorise shellfish, its arms are no adequate defence against certain fish which prey on it. The cod and the conger eel are particularly fond of it. It has, however, another method of defence, an ability to change colour very rapidly while propelling itself away from its foes, often by this means being able to make good its escape. Embedded in its skin are numerous tiny bags of pigment with muscles attached all round them. By contracting or relaxing these muscles, the octopus can vary the surface area of the pigment, and so change the colour of the body as a whole. Similar pigment cells occurring in other animals are usually controlled by the secretions of the ductless glands, and colour changes are rather slow. In the octopus they are under the direct control of the nervous system, so that the colour changes occur almost instantaneously. No other animal, not even the celebrated chameleon, is able to change its colour so rapidly as the octopus.

And now, before leaving the octopus, what can we say about the sinister creature presented to us in story and film? The common octopus has never been known to attack anyone, and certainly would have insufficient power to do much harm if it did. Larger species exist in southern seas, but normally prefer to keep in deep water, though occasional unpleasant encounters have been reported when some object in which one was hiding has been hauled aboard a small boat. It must, I think, be admitted that the octopus of fiction may be good entertainment, but is not very good natural history.

Closely related to the eight-armed octopuses are the ten-armed squids (order Teuthida) and cuttlefish (order Sepiida). In general structure they are similar to octopods, but there are significant differences both in structure and behaviour. In addition to the eight arms corresponding to those of the octopus, the squids and cuttles have two additional, much longer arms called tentacles, which are provided with suckers only towards their club-shaped tips. When not in use, these tentacles can be withdrawn into two special pouches situated at either side of the head. Squid suckers, unlike those of the octopus, are borne at the ends of short stalks, and their margins are strengthened by horny rims which in some species are serrated to give a more effective grip.

Squids and cuttles lead a much more active life than the octopus, swimming in the open seas and seldom coming into in-shore waters. Their bodies in consequence are more streamlined, and along the sides they have a pair of flat stabilising fins. Like the octopods, they can shoot rapidly through the water using their siphons. In order to escape from enemies they are able to lay their own smoke screens. Each has a bag, or ink sac, containing an inky

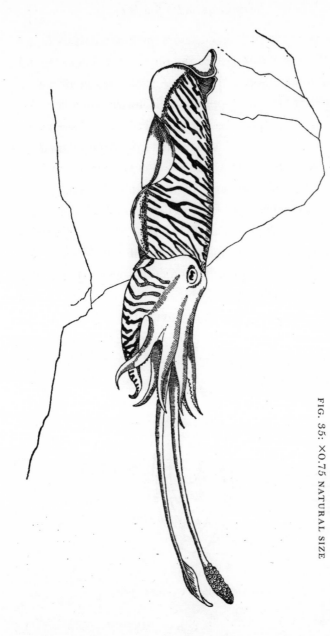

COMMON CUTTLE – *Sepia officinalis*

FIG. 35: ×0.75 NATURAL SIZE

fluid. When hard pressed, the animal shoots this liquid into the water through its siphon, putting a dense cloud between itself and its pursuer. A rapid change of colour effected by its melanophore cells further increases its chances of escape. The 'ink' contained in the sac is the sepia of the artist, and is extracted from *Sepia officinalis*, a cuttle common in British seas and in the Mediterranean, where large numbers are caught for this purpose.

Remote ancestors of the octopods and decapods had well-developed external shells. The squids and cuttles still possess the remains of this shell, not covered over by folds of the mantle. In the cuttles it is the familiar boat-shaped 'cuttlebone' which is quite common on our beaches. Cuttlefish use their spongey cuttlebones, which are filled with gas pockets, as a buoyancy device to help

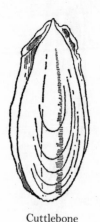

Cuttlebone

FIG. 36: ×0.25 NATURAL SIZE

them float. Before the introduction of blotting paper, cuttlebone was ground to a powder to make 'pounce' for drying ink. In squids the shell is no longer calcified, and takes the form of a long thin horny 'pen'.

Squids and cuttles are gregarious animals, often swimming in large schools. They feed on fish, and at times their abundance is a serious menace to the fishermen. In 1933 the common cuttle *Sepia officinalis* occurred in such numbers around the coasts of Scotland, following the herring shoals, that they were driven away. The mackerel fisheries along the coasts of North America are sometimes similarly affected.

One species of squid (*Todarodes sagittatus*) sometimes approaches the coast of Norway in great numbers from the deeper ocean water in pursuit of the herring shoals. On the herring they feed ravenously, and chase the fish with such vigour that hundreds of them sometimes run right up to the beach and get stranded. Large numbers of this species are occasionally stranded on British beaches.

Besides the smallish squids and cuttles, mostly of similar size to our common octopus, there exist some formidable deep-sea monsters. The largest of them are species of *Architeuthis* and *Mesonychoteuthis*, commonly known as giant and colossal squid, which with their tentacles can exceed ten or fourteen metres. They are widely distributed in the Atlantic and Pacific oceans, but are seldom encountered. They never swim into shallow in-shore waters, and those which are washed up on the beaches are always in a state of decay. Sometimes they are seen near the surface in the open ocean, apparently exhausted. Their condition is probably a result of a struggle with some other creature, possibly a whale.

That these giant squids are very powerful is known from the damage they can inflict on the large sperm whale. Large squids are the favourite food of these eighteen-metre whales, but with their formidable suckers they are not overpowered without a struggle, and the huge head and jaws of the whales often show numerous large scars made by the suckers.

All squids, cuttles and octopuses are equipped with a pair of powerful horny jaws or beaks, and it is to these that we owe the valuable ambergris found floating on the sea, and occasionally washed up on the shore. The whale is unable to digest the beaks, so they are excreted as a partially digested mass. This ambergris, or 'grey amber', is worth many pounds a gram to the manufacturers of perfumes, on account of its ability to fix various pleasant smells.

Giant squids are probably responsible for a good many of the sea-serpent stories. Although some of the monster stories may have been invented by newspapers during the 'silly season', it must be remembered that many more have been seriously recorded in all good faith. In 1877, for example, HMY *Osborne* made an official report to the

Admiralty giving details of a sea-serpent sighted off Sicily on June 2nd, and similar reports by merchant-ship captains have been numerous.

If these reports are examined, it is clear that a good many of them could be explained as the appearance of a giant squid at the surface of the sea. Twelve-metre tentacles could certainly give a serpent-like impression. Some reports, too, speak of titanic struggles between serpents and sperm whales. Undoubtedly in these cases a battle between a squid and a whale has been witnessed.

An extinct group of cephalopods, the ammonoids, were immensely diverse and abundant throughout the oceans for hundreds of millions of years. Most ammonoids had flat, spiralling shells which were divided into a series of internal chambers. They ranged in size from a coin to bigger than a tractor tyre. Fossil ammonoid shells can be found in rocks all over the world, including on many British coastlines, in particular around Lyme Bay and Lyme Regis.

Fossils of the soft body parts of ammonoids have never been found. It is generally assumed they resembled other living cephalopods, the chambered nautiluses, which have similar, divided shells. Nautiluses live in tropical seas, deep underwater. The chambers inside their shells are filled with gas, which aids their buoyancy. They swim by jet propulsion, forcing water through a siphon, as other living cephalopods do, and they have dozens of smooth, sucker-free tentacles for grabbing prey. Ammonoids may have had a similar appearance and swimming behaviour to nautiluses.

Millions of years ago ammonoids swam through the seas at the same time as the nautiluses' ancestors. But for some reason that remains unclear, the ammonoids but not the nautiluses went extinct at the same time as the dinosaurs.

11

Barnacles on the Shore

Although they are not molluscs, no survey of the shells that occur on the seashore would be complete without some reference to the little acorn barnacles. On many rocky shores they are present in greater numbers than any other animal. In areas where they are particularly abundant it is said that there may be as many as one billion of them along a 1.5 kilometre stretch of shore.

To the naturalist they are interesting because they illustrate how an animal's structure can be so modified to adapt it to a particular mode of life that it looks quite different from the more normal members of the group to which it belongs. For a long time the acorn barnacles were regarded as molluscs, because superficially they looked rather like tiny limpets, and even today many people make the same mistake. It was only when the development of their eggs was studied that it became clear that they had no connection with the molluscs, but were unusual members of the great group of crustacea, of which the shrimps, prawns, lobsters and crabs are the best-known members. The tiny larvae which hatch from the barnacle eggs were found to be unmistakably crustacean. In their subsequent development, however, they lose most of their crustacean features in becoming adapted to a sedentary life, which is an unusual method of existence for the group to which they belong.

It was Thomas Henry Huxley who first described a barnacle as a crustacean fixed by its head and kicking food into its mouth with its legs, and the best way to understand its modified structure is to trace its development from egg to adult. The way in which it differs from a typical crustacean such as a prawn or a lobster then becomes clear.

ACORN BARNACLES

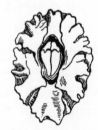

Dorsal view

Dorsal view

Semibalanus balanoides

Chthamalus stellatus

FIG. 37: ×4 NATURAL SIZE

The tiny larva which hatches from the egg is similar to that of other crustaceans but during its subsequent

development most of its crustacean features are lost.
After several weeks it acquires two tiny shell valves and
comes to look something like a tiny mussel. At this stage
it ceases its planktonic existence and sinks to the sea
bed. If it falls onto a rock or a stone on a suitable part of
the shore, development continues. But should it fall on
sand or mud, or too far up the shore or too low down, it
soon dies. The successful larva settles on its head, which
is provided with a gland producing cement. With this it
becomes firmly fixed to the spot where the remainder of
its life will be spent.

A head with eyes and feelers is very desirable for an
animal that moves about, because it enables it to seek out
its food and to avoid danger. It is less necessary to a sedentary animal. Accordingly the head of the developing
barnacle degenerates, leaving eventually little more than
a mouth and the cement gland. The tail, too, so useful to
a prawn or a lobster in moving about, is of little use to a
sedentary animal, and it likewise degenerates. The adult
barnacle thus consists in the main only of the thorax or
middle portion of the body, lying within a shell formed
from ten calcareous plates. Six of these fused together
form the sides of the shell, the other four forming a lid
which can be opened and closed.

Inside the shell the animal lies with its six pairs of
legs, many-jointed and curved, directed upwards towards
the lid. When the tide comes in, the lid opens and the

limbs are pushed out into the surrounding water, where they keep up a constant movement. They are sweeping the water for minute plankton animals, which are passed down to the mouth as they are trapped.

There are four British species of acorn barnacles, the most common and widespread being *Semibalanus balanoides.* This species normally occupies a wide zone in the middle of the shore, where they occur in immense numbers on weed-free rocks. Often the larvae settle so close together that, as they develop, many of the young barnacles die.

The position of a barnacle within the zone has a considerable effect on its subsequent life. Those that settle lower down the shore grow more quickly and reach maturity after one year, usually dying at the end of their third summer. In the upper parts of the zone, growth is slower. Spawning does not occur for the first time until they are two years old, but they usually live until their fifth year. These differences are probably connected with food supply. Barnacles living on the lower parts of the shore are covered with water for a longer time each day than those near the upper limits of the zone, and therefore have a longer time to feed. It is therefore reasonable to assume that they catch more food.

When the larvae or spat begin to settle they have been observed to search the rock surface for upwards of an hour before finally cementing themselves to the rock, presumably choosing the best situation. They always fix themselves, too, with their long axis along the direction of the flow of water, and later turn through ninety degrees. In this way they ensure that their food net, represented by their curled limbs, is set across the current of water, the best position for trapping the plankton organisms suspended in it. These limbs must be endowed with some kind of taste sense, for not only do they retract within the shell as soon as they have caught any food, in order to convey it to the mouth, but certain types of organisms, apparently distasteful to them, are not trapped. If these occur in large numbers in the water, the limbs are withdrawn and the lid closed until they have passed.

Barnacles are very sensitive to the action of waves, a factor which has a considerable effect on their distribution. On an open shore, where they are often exposed to heavy seas, barnacles flourish much more than they do on a sheltered beach. Their zone of distribution extends well above the neap high-tide mark, and well below the corresponding low-water mark. The rough water seems to provide optimum conditions for growth, the total weight of barnacles per unit area of rock surface showing a close correlation with the degree of exposure. Barnacles living on exposed rocks not only grow more quickly, but reach maturity earlier than sheltered individuals living at a similar tidal level.

Observations in the Lough Hyne district in Ireland

confirmed that these beneficial effects of exposure to wave action were connected with movement of the water. Barnacles occupying the same tidal level at three different points were examined. Inside the lough, where there was little wave action or water movement, the barnacles were small. On the coast outside, exposed to heavy seas, they were much larger, while those in the rapids connecting the lough to the sea, and where, therefore, there was a swift current but little wave action, were also large.

There are probably two distinct reasons why wave action provides optimum conditions for barnacles. In the first place there is much movement of water when the sea is rough, so that more water passes through the barnacles' food nets in a given time. This will enable them to live higher on the shore, where in calmer seas they would not be submerged long enough to catch sufficient food. For the same reason, they will be able to obtain more food and therefore to grow faster, at any level within their zone.

The extension of their zone down the shore under exposed conditions is more difficult to account for. *Semibalanus balanoides*, being a truly intertidal animal, presumably needs exposure to air for at least a part of each day as much as it needs submersion in water. Possibly the heavy surf on an exposed shore carries sufficient air down into the water in the region beyond the neap low-tide mark to make it possible for the barnacles to live there.

A third reason concerns the actual settlement of the larvae. These settle best on a rough surface, and in any case cannot settle on any rock where there is a deposit of mud or a layer of slime. Wave-swept rocks will have no mud adhering to them, nor will the small algae which give a slimy coat to sheltered rocks be able to grow there.

Barnacles are able to withstand desiccation for long periods, even in hot sunshine, their lid plates fitting very tightly when closed. Large numbers on a rocky shore can make a curious hissing noise as these lid plates rub against one another.

As with most groups of animals found on the seashore, each of the four barnacle species has its own particular zone, showing that they have different powers of resisting desiccation and immersion. Lowest of all comes *Balanus crenatus*, only occasionally exposed at low spring tide, and therefore hardly to be regarded as a true seashore species. Next comes *Perforatus perforatus*, a good deal larger but much less abundant than *Semibalanus balanoides*. It occurs low on the shore and well into the sea. The fourth species, *Chthamalus stellatus*, extends higher up the shore than *Semibalanus balanoides*, even into the splash zone, though how these latter individuals obtain enough food is a mystery.

Chthamalus is an example of a Lusitanian or Mediterranean species which is able to thrive on our western shores because of the warm water of the North Atlantic

Drift or the Gulf Stream. *Semibalanus balanoides*, on the other hand, is a true boreal or north temperate species. Where the two species occur together, as they do in the south-west, *Semibalanus* is approaching the southern limits of its distribution and *Chthamalus* the northern limits. This has a very interesting effect on their breeding. Like most marine animals, both species commence breeding when a particular temperature is reached. For *Semibalanus*, this temperature is attained in mid-winter, so that the larva or spat fall occurs in the spring. For *Chthamalus*, however, temperatures high enough to stimulate breeding activity are not reached until mid-summer, and so the spat is not ready to settle until the autumn. Further south, temperatures would remain too high all the year round for *Semibalanus* to breed, while on our east coast the water temperature would never be high enough for *Chthamalus* to breed.

Barnacles grow mostly in the spring and the late summer. Temperatures are too high in mid-summer and too low during the winter for rapid growth. During the summer, the shells of the first-year barnacles and the new growth at the base of the shell plates of older specimens appear pure white, as though bleached by the sun, whereas the shell laid down in previous years is greenish brown. During the autumn, spores of various tiny algae settle on the white shell and germinate, growing right into the shell and causing the colour change. Apparently these algae are not detrimental to the barnacles. In fact they may help to supply them with oxygen. When the sun shines on the water, numerous oxygen bubbles can often be seen streaming up from the shell, the result of photosynthesis in the algae.

Besides rocks and stones, any suitable hard surface within the zone of distribution may carry its colony of barnacles. Mollusc shells provide an excellent surface for attachment, while crabs are frequently found carrying barnacles on their shells, as well as other sedentary animals. Luckily for them, the crabs can cast off these lodgers every year when they moult, or they might eventually find themselves very overburdened.

One of the latest additions to the British fauna is an Australian barnacle, *Austrominius modestus*. It was first noted in 1947, since when it has been spreading rapidly along the south coast. Presumably it came into our waters attached to a ship which had come from Australia, and found conditions here suitable for breeding.

There is another kind of barnacle which you may find on the shore. This is the stalked or ship's barnacle, sometimes washed up attached to driftwood. Like the acorn barnacles, it leads a sedentary life attached by its head to the bottoms of ships. Although the sense organs are lost, the head is retained and enlarged to form a stalk several centimetres long and serving to hold the rest of the body away from the ship. As with the acorn barnacle, it is the

STALKED BARNACLE
Lepas anatifera

FIG. 38: NATURAL SIZE

thorax which forms the functional part of the adult and carries six pairs of limbs to comb the water for food. The shell enclosing it consists of five calcareous plates.

Stalked barnacles have always been a nuisance to shipping. They are capable of settling and developing in such numbers that within a few months from launching, or cleaning, the whole bottom of a ship may be covered with them, and its speed be appreciably reduced. Dry docking to remove this growth is necessary at regular intervals if the efficiency of vessels is to be maintained. Six months after scraping, a battleship of 35,000 tons can have its speed reduced by at least one knot through new growth.

In earlier times natural history was a curious mixture of observed facts and myths, and many of the best naturalists seemed incapable of separating the two. In fact the myths were sometimes quoted as personal observations. One of the most famous of these medieval myths was that which credited the stalked barnacle with being the progenitor of the barnacle or bernicle goose.

Sir John Mandeville, a fifteenth-century traveller, claimed to have made a special study of this remarkable transformation. 'There is a small island in Lancashire,' he wrote,

wherein we find broken pieces of old and bruised ships which have been cast thither by shipwrake, whereon is found a certain spume or froth which in time changeth into a certain shell like that of a muskle, but sharper pointed, wherein is a thing in form like fine woven silk. When perfectly formed the shel gapeth open, and there appeareth the legs of a bird. As it groweth bigger it all cometh forth till at length it hangeth only by the bill. In a short space of time it cometh to maturity, and falleth into the sea, where it gathereth feathers and groweth to a fowl, bigger than a mallard and lesser than a goose, which the people speak of by no other name than the tree goose, and of which a good one can be bought for three pence.

Perhaps he felt the story might be difficult for some people to believe, for he added, 'of that which we have seen and handled, of that do we testify'. His powers of observation must indeed have been remarkable!

Some Practical Hints for Collecting and Photographing Shell Life

There is great fun to be had in finding all kinds of shell life on the shore, but many people will want to do more than this. Some will want to make collections either of the shells they find or of the complete animals preserved in their shells. Others may like to keep their findings alive for a few days in order to study them in action, while some again may be keen photographers anxious to build up a collection of photographs showing various kinds of seashore molluscs alive in their natural surroundings.

COLLECTING SHELL LIFE

Whatever your particular interests, you will need to search the shore intelligently and methodically if you are to find the maximum number of species, remembering that the distribution of shore molluscs depends both upon the zone, which is most easily identified by means of the type of seaweed found growing there, and upon the shore material. Rocks, rock pools, sand, gravel and mud all have their characteristic mollusc populations. Once the collector has grasped the full significance of these two factors, they will be in a favourable position for finding the maximum number of species.

Many species live so far down the shore that they remain covered altogether except during the few days of each spring tide, and even then they will be exposed for only an hour or so at each tide. The most profitable time of all, then, for hunting seashore creatures is the hour or so around spring-tide low water. In different parts of the country these low spring tides occur at different parts of the day.

If you are going to search the lowest parts of the shore you should be there at least half an hour before low water to give yourself the maximum amount of time. Once the tide has turned, keep a sharp lookout, because spring tides come in very rapidly and you may easily be cut off.

Little in the way of equipment is required for collecting shell life, beyond one or more jars in which the specimens can be stored until they are sorted out at home, and a notebook. In this, each specimen should be recorded, with as much detail about the position where it was found as possible. The zone in which it was living and the type of ground, whether it was exposed or buried, covered with seaweed or living beneath a rock or a stone – all this information should be noted at the time. Eventually it can be transferred to the label when the specimen is finally added to your collection.

All this of course applies to shells found complete with their living occupants. Empty shells, of which you will find plenty strewn about the beach, may have been moved considerable distances by the action of the waves, so where you find them is no guide to where they actually lived. Many of them, of course, will have been washed in from the shallow offshore waters where they live either on or buried in the sea bed.

In your hunting, too, do not forget the burrowing species. To expose these you will need a spade, and remember that your richest haul is likely well down the shore, especially where there is mud or muddy sand or gravel.

Be careful not to disturb other marine life while you are collecting shells. If you turn over rocks, always return them to their original position because there may well be animals seeking shelter underneath. Be careful not to trample across delicate habitats on the beach and be mindful of the number of shells you are taking. Leave some for the next shell collectors who come along after you.

To obtain perfect shells that haven't been worn by the waves, some shell collectors choose to take living molluscs then either preserve the animal, shell and all, in preserving fluids, or extract the body (usually after boiling the mollusc) and just keep the shell. If you decide to take this approach to shell collecting, always take note of any local regulations that may limit the daily number and minimum size of living shells that can be collected, and don't collect inside nature reserves or protected areas. Or you may decide to leave the living molluscs where they are and perhaps just take photographs home with you instead.

A TEMPORARY AQUARIUM

Before killing and preserving your specimens or their shells you might like to keep them alive for a few days to observe their ways. For this you will need a small rectangular tank, covering the bottom with six or seven centimetres of sand brought up from a part of the shore which is washed by the sea every day, or washed gravel, if you are collecting on a gravel shore. Collect also a few larger stones, preferably some you have found with specimens attached to them. Fill your tank with sea water and aerate the water with an air pump. Put in a few plants of some of the smaller kinds of seaweeds for additional aeration. These can usually be collected attached to small stones or pieces of rock.

PRESERVING SHELLS

When collecting shells, it may be necessary to remove their animals. This can be done in several ways. With bivalves the simplest way is to cut through the adductor muscles, which anchor the animals to their shells, using a sharp knife or razor blade. Gastropods can be killed by immersing them in boiling water for a minute or two and then extracting them with a pin by the time-honoured method used for extracting winkles from their shells.

After the animals have been removed, the shells should be thoroughly washed using a small brush, and then placed in a dilute solution of household bleach for an hour or two to remove any stains. The bleach will not affect the natural colouring of the shell. After rinsing, the shells must be laid out to dry.

Malacologists usually keep shells in cabinets with shallow drawers, with multiple shells of the same species kept together either in small plastic bags or in small cardboard boxes.

PHOTOGRAPHING SHELL LIFE

An alternative to collecting molluscs and their shells is to build up a collection of photographs. Taking pictures of molluscs in their natural surroundings is a fascinating hobby and it is not as difficult as you might imagine. The equipment to take good images has never been more easily or cheaply available.

Smartphone cameras can take excellent pictures of molluscs, and some phones are waterproof or splash-proof, so they can be immersed in tide pools to get underwater shots. (Don't forget to rinse your phone in fresh water afterwards.)

Macro lens adaptors are available for many smartphones, allowing you to take close-up shots of very small shells. Microscope attachments for smartphones will help you take shots of even tinier shells.

Any other digital camera can be used to photograph molluscs. Waterproof compact cameras are also widely available and cheaper than ever. Some have inbuilt settings for underwater photographs and macro shots.

When shooting in water, try not to disturb sediments at the bottom as you reach in – the clearer the water, the clearer your image. Good results are often obtained by shooting upwards, towards the surface.

If you take clear photographs (including an indication of scale, using a ruler or a coin in shot), you can leave the animals and their shells behind on the beach; once back at home, you can use the images to identify which species you found.

Mollusc Classification

In the classification of animals the largest groups are called phyla, and each phylum contains a large number of animals all built upon the same general plan, but within the phylum there are many smaller groups showing considerable differences from each other. The members of a phylum are further divided into classes, and these in turn into subclasses, orders and families. Each family consists of one or more genera, and each genus contains its complement of species.

There are somewhere in the region of eighty thousand named mollusc species living the oceans, in fresh waters and on land today, and many more that are yet to be found and identified. This makes them the second most diverse phylum of animals on Earth, after the arthropods (which includes insects and crustaceans). With so many species, the task of classifying the molluscs and working out the evolutionary relationships between them all is a major challenge. To complicate matters, experts are undecided on the major evolutionary events in the mollusc lineage and it is not widely accepted what the first molluscs looked like or indeed when and how each group of molluscs evolved. It is generally agreed that the mollusc phylum has existed for at least 500 million years and in that time a myriad of subgroups and species have evolved and become extinct.

In the following classification of the phylum Mollusca the only families shown are those with representatives which are broadly dealt with in this book, so that it is not a complete classification of all the molluscs to be found in the world. Against each class, subclass, order or family, as appropriate, the number of the chapter in which it is dealt with is shown. A summary of the main characteristics of each class, subclass and order is given.

Class POLYPLACOPHORA (1)

The Chitons, with a shell made from eight separate calcareous plates; they have elongated limpet-like bodies with a well-developed foot and a head lacking tentacles; the mantle forms a fringe encircling the foot; there are many pairs of ctenidia or gills. With their flexible shells, chitons can roll up in a ball for protection, in a similar way to woodlice.

Family Lepidochitonidae
Lepidochitona cinerea – common or grey chiton

Class GASTROPODA

Molluscs with a single, usually coiled, shell; a well-developed head with one or two pairs of tentacles, and usually a pair of eyes; a well-developed flat muscular foot used in most species for creeping. This is the biggest mollusc class with at least forty thousand species, and the only group of molluscs that has successfully colonised land. With so many species, the gastropods pose a perennial challenge for taxonomists. In 2017, a revised five-hundred-page gastropod classification was published which divides the gastropods into five main subclasses: the PATELLOGASTROPODA, the true limpets; the VETIGASTROPODA, an ancient lineage of sea snails characterised by the intersected structure of their shells; the NERITIMORPHA, a highly diverse group including snails with spiral, conical or limpet-like shells, as well as slug-like forms, living everywhere from deep hydrothermal vents to trees on land; the CAENOGASTROPODA, including more than half of all living gastropods, which all exhibit complete torsion of 180 degrees; and the HETEROBRANCHIA, including former subclasses the Opisthobranchs (various types of sea-slugs with a reduced or no shell) and Pulmonates (air-breathing slugs and snails). Outside these five subclasses, there are also some less well-known groups of deep-sea gastropods.

Subclass PATELLOGASTROPODA (1)

Family Lottidae
Tectura virginea – white tortoiseshell limpet
Testudinalia testudinalis – tortoiseshell limpet
Family Patellidae
Patella pellucida – blue-rayed limpet
Patella vulgata – common limpet

Subclass VETIGASTROPODA

Family Fissurellidae (1)
Diodora graeca – keyhole limpet
Family Phasianellidae (2)
Tricolia pullus – pheasant shell
Family Trochidae (2)
Calliostoma zizyphinum – painted top shell
Phorcus lineatus – thick top shell
Steromphala cineraria – grey top shell
Steromphala umbilicalis – flat top shell

Subclass NERITIMORPHA

Family Neritidae
Theodoxus fluviatilis – river nerite

Subclass CAENOGASTROPODA

Family Barleeiidae
Barleeia species
Family Bithyniidae
Bithynia – mud bithynia or faucet snail
Family Buccinidae (3)
Buccinum undatum – common whelk
Family Calyptraeidae (3)
Crepidula fornicata – slipper limpet
Family Cerithiidae (2)
Bittium reticulatum – needlewhelk
Family Epitoniidae (2)
Epitonium clathrus – wentletrap
Family Hydrobiidae
Hydrobia – spire snail or mud snail
Family Littorinidae (2)
Lacuna vincta – banded chink shell
Littorina littorea – common periwinkle
Littorina obtusata – flat periwinkle
Littorina saxatilis – rough periwinkle
Melarhaphe neritoides – small periwinkle
Family Muricidae (3)
Nucella lapillus – dog whelk
Ocenebra erinaceus – sting winkle
Urosalpinx cinerea – oyster drill
Family Nassariidae (3)
Tritia incrassata – thick-lipped dog whelk
Tritia reticulata – netted dog whelk
Family Naticidae (3)
Euspira catena – necklace shell
Euspira pallida – pale moon snail

Family Rissoidae (2)
Cingula species
Rissoa species – spire shells
Family Triphoridae (2)
Monophorus perversus – reversed horn shell
Family Triviidae (3)
Trivia monacha – spotted cowrie
Family Turridae (3)
Conelets
Family Valvatidae
Valvata species – valve shells
Family Velutinidae (3)
Lamellaria species – velvet shells
Family Viviparidae
Viviparus species – river snails

Subclass HETEROBRANCHIA

Family Acteonidae (has not been assigned to an order yet)
Acteon tornatilis – bubble shell (4)

ORDER CEPHALASPIDAE (4)
Family Haminoeidae
Haminoea hydatis and elegans – bubble shells
Family Philinidae
Philine aperta – lobe shell
Family Retusidae
Retusa obtusa – blunt bubble shell or Arctic barrel-bubble

ORDER APLYSIIDA (4)
Family Akeridae
Akera bullata – soft bubble shell or royal flush sea-slug
Family Aplysiidae
Aplysia punctata – sea-hare

ORDER NUDIBRANCHIA (4)

Marine gastropods that have no shells as adults. Nudibranchs have simple eyes that can discern light and dark. The word nudibranch comes from Greek and Latin words meaning naked gills. They breathe through external gills; in some nudibranchs the gills are feathery plumes surrounding the anus, and some have numerous finger-like projections called cerata which also act as gills. At the front end, club-shaped rhinophores detect chemical odours in the water.

Family Dendronotidae
Dendronosus frondosus – bushy-backed sea-slug
Family Dorididae
Doris pseudoargus – sea-lemon
Aeolidia papillosa – grey sea-slug

SUPERORDER HYGROPHILA

Air-breathing freshwater snails and limpets, with eyes at the base of their tentacles and thin, translucent shells.
Family Lymnaeidae
Myxas species – pond snails
Family Physidae
Physa fontinalis – bladder snail
Family Planorbidae
Ancylus species – freshwater limpets
Planorbis species – ram's horn snails

ORDER STYLOMMATOPHORA

Terrestrial, air-breathing snails and slugs with eyes at the tips of the hind pair of tentacles.
Family Arionidae
Arion – roundback slugs

Family Azecidae

Azeca goodalli – three-toothed moss snail

Family Clausiliidae

Balea perversa – tree snail

Clausilia species – door snails

Family Cochlicopidae

Cochlicopa lubrica – slippery moss snail

Family Enidae

Ena montana – mountain bulin

Family Helicadae

Helix species – typical land snails

Family Limacidae

Limax species – true slugs

Family Oxychilidae

Oxychilus draparnaudi – Draparnaud's glass snail

Family Pupillidae

Pupilla species – chrysalis snails

Family Testacellidae

Testacella species – shelled slugs

Family Vitrinidae

Vitrina pellucida – pellucid glass snail

Class BIVALVIA

Bivalve molluscs have characteristic twinned shells. They have no head and their gills form extensive plates for filtering food particles from sea water. Like the gastropods, they are difficult to classify. A recent update of bivalve taxonomy, from 2010, divides them into eighteen orders (including many that are extinct and only known from fossils), and four subclasses. Some bivalves are fixed to rocks or the sea bed by byssus threads or some other means such as a cement-like glue. Some are free-living and either lie on the surface of the sea bed or burrow actively through sand or mud. There are also bivalves that dig deep holes in the sea bed, rock and wood.

ORDER MYTILIDA (5)
Family Mytilidae
Modiolula phaseolina – bean horse mussel
Modiolus barbatus – bearded horse mussel
Modiolus modiolus – horse mussel
Mytilus edulis – common mussel, blue mussel

ORDER ARCIDA (5)
Family Arcidae
Arca tetragona – ark shell

ORDER PTERIIDA (5)
Family Pinnidae
Atrina fragilis – fan mussel
Family Pteridae (6)
Pinctada species – pearl oysters

ORDER OSTREIDA (6)
Family Ostreidae
Magallana angulata – Pacific oyster or Portuguese oyster
Ostrea edulis – native oyster
Ostrea virginica – eastern oyster, American oyster or
    Virginia oyster

ORDER PECTINIDA (6)
Family Anomiidae
Anomia ephippium – saddle oyster
Family Pectinidae
Aequipecten opercularis – queen scallop or quin

Mimachlamys varia – variegated scallop
Pecten maximus – great scallop or edible scallop
Talochlamys pusio – humpback scallop

ORDER LIMIDA (6)
Family Limidae
Limaria hians – gaping file shell

ORDER UNIONIDA (5)
Family Unionidae
Anodonta anatina – duck mussel
Anodonta cygnea – swan mussel
Margaritifera margaritifera – pearl mussel
Unio pictorum – painter's mussel
Unio tumidus – swollen river mussel

ORDER VENERIDA
Family Arctidae (8)
Arctica islandica – ocean quahog
Family Cardiidae (7)
Acanthocardia aculeata – spiny cockle
Acanthocardia echinata – prickly cockle
Acanthocardia tuberculata – rough cockle
Cerastoderma edule – common cockle
Corculum cardissa – heart cockle
Laevicardium crassum – smooth cockle
Parvicardium exiguum – little cockle
Parvicardium pinnulatum – banded cockle
Parvicardium scabrum – knotted cockle
Family Donacidae (8)
Donax species – wedge shells or bean clams
Family Dreissenidae (5)
Dreissena polymorpha – zebra mussel

Family Lasaeidae (8)

Kellia suborbicularis

Lasaea rubra

Lepton squamosum – coin shell

Montacuta species – Montagu shells

Family Lucinidae (8)

Lucinoma borealis – northern lucina

Family Mactridae (9)

Lutraria species – otter shells

Spisula and *Mactra* species – trough shells or duck clams

Family Pharidae (9)

Ensis species – razor shells

Family Pisidiidae (7)

Pisidium species – pea clams or pill clams

Family Psammobiidae (8)

Gari species – sunset shells

Family Semelidae (8)

Abra species – furrow shells

Scrobicularia species – furrow shells

Family Solenidae (9)

Solen species – razor shells

Family Sphaeriidae (7)

Sphaerium – fingernail cockles or orb-shell cockles

Family Tellinidae (8)

Macoma balthica – Baltic clam or Baltic tellin

Tellina species – tellins

Family Ungulinidae (8)

Diplodonta rotundata

Family Veneridae (8)

Callista chione – smooth venus

Chamelea striatula – striped venus

Clausinella fasciata – banded venus

Dosinia exoleta – rayed artemis

Dosinia lupinus – smooth artemis

Mercenaria mercenaria – hard-shell clam

Mysia undata – wavy venus

Petricolaria pholadiformis – false angel wing, American piddock or American rock-borer

Timoclea ovata – oval venus

Venerupis species – carpet shells

Venus species – venus shells

ORDER MYIDA (9)
Family Hiatellidae

Hiatella species

Family Myidae

Mya arenaria – sand or common gaper

Mya truncata – blunt gaper

Family Pholadidae

Barnea candida – white piddock

Barnea parva – little piddock

Pholadidea loscombiana – paper piddock

Pholas dactylus – common piddock

Xylophaga dorsalis – wood-borer

Zirfaea crispata – oval piddock

Family Teredinidae

Nototeredo norvagica – Norway shipworm

Psiloteredo megotara – big-ear shipworm or drifting shipworm

Teredo navalis – shipworm

Class SCAPHOPODA (4)

A small class of molluscs, known as tusk shells.
Family Dentaliidae
Antalis entalis – elephant's tusk shell

Class CEPHALOPODA (10)

ORDER OCTOPODA
Eight-armed octopuses

ORDER VAMPYROMORPHIDA
Vampire squid

ORDER TEUTHIDA
 Squid

ORDER SEPIOLIDA
Pygmy and bobtail squid

ORDER SEPIIDA
Cuttlefish

ORDER SPIRULIDA
Ram's horn squid

ORDER NAUTILIDA
Nautiluses

Index

Index